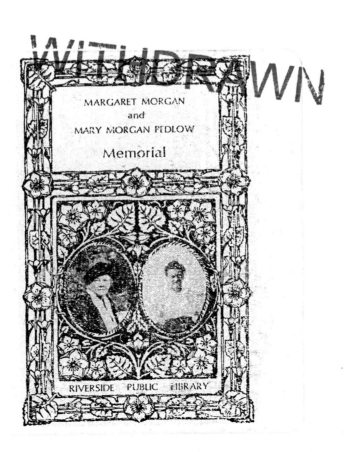

MARGARET MORGAN
and
MARY MORGAN PEDLOW

Memorial

Rosa Parks

CIVIL RIGHTS LEADER

Black Americans of Achievement

LEGACY EDITION

Muhammad Ali

Frederick Douglass

W.E.B. Du Bois

Marcus Garvey

Alex Haley

Langston Hughes

Jesse Jackson

Coretta Scott King

Martin Luther King, Jr.

Malcolm X

Thurgood Marshall

Jesse Owens

Rosa Parks

Colin Powell

Sojourner Truth

Harriet Tubman

Nat Turner

Booker T. Washington

Black Americans of Achievement

LEGACY EDITION

Rosa Parks

CIVIL RIGHTS LEADER

Mary Hull

With additional text written by
Gloria Blakely

Consulting Editor, Revised Edition
Heather Lehr Wagner

Senior Consulting Editor, First Edition
Nathan Irvin Huggins
Director, W.E.B. Du Bois Institute
for Afro-American Research
Harvard University

CHELSEA HOUSE
PUBLISHERS
A Haights Cross Communications Company
Philadelphia

COVER: Civil rights pioneer Rosa Parks smiles during a ceremony held on Capitol Hill in 1999 to present her with the Congressional Gold Medal.

CHELSEA HOUSE PUBLISHERS

VP, NEW PRODUCT DEVELOPMENT Sally Cheney
DIRECTOR OF PRODUCTION Kim Shinners
CREATIVE MANAGER Takeshi Takahashi
MANUFACTURING MANAGER Diann Grasse

Staff for ROSA PARKS

EXECUTIVE EDITOR Lee Marcott
ASSISTANT EDITOR Alexis Browsh
PRODUCTION EDITOR Noelle Nardone
PHOTO EDITOR Sarah Bloom
SERIES AND COVER DESIGNER Keith Trego
LAYOUT 21st Century Publishing and Communications, Inc.

©2005 by Chelsea House Publishers,
a subsidiary of Haights Cross Communications.
All rights reserved. Printed and bound in the United States of America.

A Haights Cross Communications ✦ Company

www.chelseahouse.com

First Printing

9 8 7 6 5 4 3 2 1

Library of Congress Cataloging-in-Publication Data

Hull, Mary.
    Rosa Parks : civil rights leader / Mary Hull; with additional text by Gloria Blakely.
        p. cm.—(Black Americans of achievement)
Includes bibliographical references and index.
    ISBN 0-7910-8164-8 (hardcover) — ISBN 0-7910-8338-1 (pbk.)
    1. Parks, Rosa, 1913–   —Juvenile literature. 2. African Americans—Alabama—Montgomery—
Biography—Juvenile literature. 3. Civil rights workers—Alabama—Montgomery—Biography—
Juvenile literature. 4. African Americans—Civil rights—Alabama—Montgomery—Juvenile
literature. 5. Segregation in transportation—Alabama—Montgomery—History—20th
century—Juvenile literature. 6. Montgomery (Ala.)—Race relations—Juvenile literature.
7. Montgomery (Ala.)—Biography—Juvenile literature. I. Title. II. Series.
F334.M753P374 2004

2004016521

Contents

Introduction

Nearly 20 years ago, Chelsea House Publishers began to publish the first volumes in the series called BLACK AMERICANS OF ACHIEVEMENT. This series eventually numbered over a hundred books and profiled outstanding African Americans from many walks of life. Today, if you ask school teachers and school librarians what comes to mind when you mention Chelsea House, many will say—"Black Americans of Achievement."

The mix of individuals whose lives we covered was eclectic, to say the least. Some were well known—Muhammad Ali and Dr. Martin Luther King, Jr, for example. But others, such as Harriet Tubman and Sojourner Truth, were lesser-known figures who were introduced to modern readers through these books. The individuals profiled were chosen for their actions, their deeds, and ultimately their influence on the lives of others and their impact on our nation as a whole. By sharing these stories of unique Americans, we hoped to illustrate how ordinary individuals can be transformed by extraordinary circumstances to become people of greatness. We also hoped that these special stories would encourage young-adult readers to make their own contribution to a better world. Judging from the many wonderful letters we have received about the BLACK AMERICANS OF ACHIEVEMENT biographies over the years from students, librarians, and teachers, they have certainly fulfilled the goal of inspiring others!

Now, some 20 years later, we are publishing 18 volumes of the original BLACK AMERICANS OF ACHIEVEMENT series in revised editions to bring the books into the twenty-first century and make them available to a new generation of young-adult readers. The selection was based on the importance of these figures to American life and the popularity of the original books with our readers. These revised editions have a new full-color design and, wherever possible, we have added color photographs. The books have new features, including quotes from the writings and speeches of leaders and interesting and unusual facts about their lives. The concluding section of each book gives new emphasis to the legacy of these men and women for the current generation of readers.

The lives of these African-American leaders are unique and remarkable. By transcending the barriers that racism placed in their paths, they are examples of the power and resiliency of the human spirit and are an inspiration to readers.

We present these wonderful books to our audience for their reading pleasure.

Lee M. Marcott
Chelsea House Publishers
August 2004

"The Straw that Broke the Camel's Back"

Even for Montgomery, Alabama, where temperatures seldom fall below 40 degrees in the coldest months of winter, it was unusually hot on the first day of December 1955. It was nearly 5:30 P.M. when Rosa Parks put away the piles of new suits she was working on and left her job at the Montgomery Fair department store to board a bus for home. The petite, bespectacled woman had been raising and lowering hemlines, altering waistbands, and adjusting sleeve lengths all day at her job as a tailor's assistant in the alterations department of the store. The holiday season was the busiest time of year for store workers, and this afternoon she was tired and her shoulders ached from bending over her sewing machine. As Rosa walked the half-block from the department store to the bus stop at Court Square, passing beneath the city's Christmas decorations, she was thinking of all the work she still had to do at home that night.

The square was decorated with red and green Christmas lights, and a large banner hung from one of the storefronts, pronouncing "Peace On Earth, Goodwill To Men." Court Square in Montgomery, Alabama—the "Cradle of the Confederacy"—was a historic place. In 1861, Jefferson Davis's inauguration as president of the Confederacy had taken place there, and slave auctions had been held on the site before the Civil War.

The Thirteenth Amendment had outlawed slavery in 1865, but many white southerners had never been able to regard blacks as their equals or even as citizens of the United States. Slavery was replaced by segregation—laws and practices mandating the exclusion of blacks from the rest of society. Under segregation, black children could not go to the same schools as white children, and blacks were not allowed to use the same public facilities (hotels, theaters, restaurants, lunch counters, sinks, bathrooms, water fountains, waiting rooms, libraries, parks, swimming pools, etc.) as white people. Southern courtrooms even had separate "colored" and "white" Bibles to use when swearing in witnesses. Blacks were also not allowed the same access to public transportation as whites.

As long as the separate facilities provided for blacks were equal to those provided for whites, the Supreme Court had ruled in 1896 in *Plessy* v. *Ferguson,* the states were free to enact these so-called Jim Crow laws. Of course, in practice, black facilities were never equal, and segregation served exactly the purpose that its creators intended—to enforce upon blacks the constant message that they were second-class citizens.

KNOWING HER PLACE

When the Cleveland Avenue bus pulled over to its stop at Court Square on that warm Thursday afternoon in 1955, Rosa Parks noticed that there were passengers standing inside, so she let the bus pass her by with the hope that the next one would be less crowded. While she waited for it to come along, she crossed the street and did some shopping. When she returned to the square with her shopping bag, a Cleveland Avenue bus stopped. Since no one appeared to be standing inside, she paid the ten-cent fare, boarded, and sat down in the first vacant seat she saw, the eleventh seat back, on the aisle, immediately behind the whites-only section of the bus. A black man occupied the window seat to her right; two black women sat in the seats across the aisle to her left.

The first 10 seats of every Montgomery city bus were reserved for white people only. Even if, as frequently happened, the bus was filled with only black passengers, to the extent that people were standing in the aisles, blacks were not to use these seats. (This differed from the practice in most other southern cities, where blacks would fill seats from the rear forward and whites from the front back; if no white passengers boarded on a particular route, blacks could occupy every seat on the bus.) Under the letter of the Montgomery city law, blacks could sit anywhere behind this whites-only section; they could be compelled to surrender their seat for a white passenger only if another was available. Alabama state law, however, gave bus drivers virtually unlimited discretion in enforcing segregation on their buses, and black passengers in Montgomery were frequently ordered to the rear of the bus to make way for white passengers once the whites-only section was filled to capacity. Often an entire row of black passengers was forced to stand or move rearward in order to free a single seat for a white rider, as segregation statutes prohibited a white and a black from sitting next to or even across the aisle from one another.

Many Montgomery bus drivers extended this kind of discrimination to their general treatment of black passengers. Although blacks paid the same bus fare as whites, many drivers did not extend them the same courtesies. For instance, drivers always picked up white passengers at every block, but they usually picked up black passengers at every other block. Some drivers forced blacks to enter their buses through the rear door; often, a black would pay his fare to the driver up front and disembark to reenter through the back door, only to have the driver take off before he or she was able to get back on.

Happy and relieved to have found a seat, Parks sat with her purse and shopping bag in her lap, thinking of the work still ahead of her at home, where she would prepare the letters she had to mail as part of her responsibilities as the volunteer secretary for the Montgomery branch of the NAACP (National Association for the Advancement of Colored People), the nation's oldest and most prominent civil rights organization. By now, she thought, her husband, Raymond, would already be home preparing their supper of ham and collard greens. He would be expecting her soon.

On the third stop after she was aboard, the bus pulled over at the Empire Theater and six whites entered and filled the open front seats. One white man was left standing. Although he did not raise any objection and stood quietly, the driver noticed that he was without a seat. Immediately, the driver, a portly man named J.F. Blake, ordered the four blacks in the sixth row to move from the area, regarded sometimes as the neutral middle, so the white man could sit down without being in the same row as a black person. This order went beyond Montgomery's segregation laws, but Blake exerted free reign.

"All right, you folks, I want those seats," he yelled back to them. (These words, quoted from David Garrow's *Bearing the Cross*, represent the politer of the many existing versions of what the bus driver said on that fateful day. According to the Reverend Ralph Abernathy, for example, in his autobiography *And the Walls Came Tumbling Down*, the driver referred to the four passengers he was addressing as "niggers," not "folks.") For a second, nobody moved. "Y'all better make it light on yourselves and let me have those seats," the driver yelled. The man to Parks's right stood up to move. She shifted her legs to

Rosa Parks smiling after the Supreme Court ruled segregation on public city transportation illegal. The ruling came down in December 1956, two years after Parks challenged southern society and segregation on December 1, 1954, by refusing to give up her seat on a Montgomery, Alabama, bus.

let him pass and then she herself moved—to the seat next to the window. The two women across the aisle got up.

Seeing that Parks was still sitting the driver walked back, stood over her and repeated his order: "Look, woman, I told you I wanted the seat. Are you going to stand up?" Parks said, "No, I'm not." He told her he would call the police if she did not move. "You may do that," she answered. Blake left the bus angrily and went for the police. Several passengers—all of them black—asked for transfers, reluctant to become involved in an incident that invited trouble with whites. While everyone else aboard the bus waited to see what would happen next, Parks looked out the window at Montgomery. The bus grew very quiet.

Parks had a right to be scared, for she recognized the driver. Twelve years earlier, she had paid in the front but refused to reenter the bus through the rear door and had been evicted from the vehicle by this same driver. Although Parks had seen him before while waiting at bus stops, she never boarded a bus if she knew he was driving. In all these years she had never forgotten his face. That evening, Parks had not looked at the driver when she boarded, but when he stood over her, there was no mistaking who he was.

Parks's mother and grandparents had always taught her not to regard herself as inferior to whites because she was black, but she admitted that until that fateful December day on the bus "every part of my life pointed to the white superiority and negro inferiority." She was uncertain about what exactly had provoked her not to move on the bus driver's order. She was certainly tired and her shoulders ached, but no more than usual after a long day. Certainly she had seen and personally felt the insults of local bus drivers before, still the familiar arrogant racist manner became too much to tolerate. "I had had enough," Parks later said. She was tired of giving in. "I wanted to be treated like a human being. I knew someone had to take the first step, and I made up my mind not to move."

THE ARREST

Two policemen returned with Blake to the bus. The driver pointed to Parks and said, "That one won't stand up." After one officer asked if the driver had requested her to rise, he then questioned, "Why don't you stand up?"

"Why do you push us around?" Parks responded with a question of her own as the policemen approached. "I don't know," the officer said, "but the law is the law, and you're under arrest." One officer took Parks's purse, and the other took her shopping bag while she was led off the bus. As they left, an officer asked Blake if he wanted to press charges. "Yes," said the driver. He would finish his route before going to city hall to swear out and sign an arrest warrant, until then Parks was held in custody.

Parks rode alone in the back of the police car to Montgomery City Hall. On the drive an officer repeated the query about why she didn't stand when asked. She held her silence. In city hall she passed a fountain and asked if she could have some water. A different policeman stopped her just as she bent to take a sip. A simple drink of water too was denied her until she reached her jail cell. Heading to the processing area the police took her belongings again, asked her if there was anything in her pockets, and questioned her as to whether she was drunk, unable to believe that any respectable, sober woman would challenge white authority as Parks had done. Indeed, the timid-looking, 42-year-old seamstress seemed an unlikely candidate for defying the segregation laws; in doing so, she was challenging the very nature of southern society. "I've always been timid," Parks later said of herself, "but my entire life has demanded of me that I be courageous." She was a determined woman with no great fear or anger that day.

She was fingerprinted and mug shots were taken before being led to her cell by a white matron. City police arrested Parks on charges of violating the segregation laws of Montgomery, but the city prosecutor, recognizing that technically Parks had not violated the city ordinance, decided that the arrest should be based on the segregation laws of the state of Alabama instead, a more serious offense. Parks was not allowed to call her husband until she was photographed and fingerprinted. She remembered later that it hurt when they pulled her fingernails to make the prints. Then they placed her in a cell by herself, though the matron moved her to a cell with two other women, explaining that this way she would not be as lonely.

One of her cellmates ignored her, but the other told her that she was in jail for attacking her boyfriend with an ax. The woman said she had acted in self-defense because her boyfriend was trying to hurt her. After listening to the woman's story, Parks wanted to help. The matron interrupted their conversation though.

Parks was finally allowed to make a call after indicating, in writing, whom she was telephoning. The matron gave her a dime for the public phone booth and remained nearby listening. Parks's mother answered the phone at home. "Did they beat you?" she wanted to know as soon as she heard her daughter was in jail. Parks assured her mother that she was alright, and then spoke to Ray, who told her he would be right over. Since they did not own a car, Parks knew it could take Ray a while to find a ride, but as they were talking a friend, who heard the news of her arrest, came by and offered Ray a lift to the police station.

Parks was then escorted back to her cell where she resumed the conversation with her cellmate. The woman began writing down the phone numbers of her two brothers on a scrap of paper and asked Parks to call them for her, as she had not been allowed to contact them from the jail.

Meanwhile, unknown to Parks, someone who saw her arrest had called Edgar Daniel Nixon, the former leader of the Montgomery NAACP and the city's most prominent black activist. Parks and E.D. Nixon, as his friends called him, had known each other since she joined the organization in 1943. For 12 years, Parks had worked for Nixon as a volunteer secretary, arranging meetings, convening with people, and keeping members notified about current events. She had also worked closely with him in the Montgomery Voters League, an organization that encouraged blacks to register to vote.

(For additional information on Nixon, enter "E.D. Nixon" into any search engine and browse the sites listed.)

As soon as Nixon learned of Parks's arrest, he telephoned the police station to ask what the charge was. "It's none of your goddamned business," the officer who answered his call told him and hung up the phone. Nixon, unable to reach African-American attorney Fred Gray, called some white friends of the Parkses and him, Clifford and Virginia Durr. Clifford Durr, a lawyer with some influence in Montgomery, who had known the Parkses for several years, called the police station and found out that Parks had been arrested under the segregation laws. The Durrs drove Nixon to the police station and posted a $100 bond in exchange for Parks's release. The matron came to take Parks away before her cell mate could give her the phone numbers she had written down, so, as Parks was being escorted out of the jail, the woman crumpled the piece of paper and threw it down the hall and through the open iron mesh door. The paper landed right in front of Parks's feet; she picked it up and put it in her pocket.

After two hours in the cell, Parks was glad to see Nixon and the Durrs. At the sight of Rosa, Virginia Durr hugged away her own fears for Parks's safety. As they left the police station, Ray Parks and a white friend were just driving up. They all returned to the Parkses' home in the black section of Montgomery, where they discussed the arrest in Ray and Rosa's living room. Her trial was set for the upcoming Monday, December 5.

READY TO BREAK JIM CROW

Nixon had been looking for a chance to test the segregation laws of Montgomery and Alabama in court, and he regarded Parks's arrest as a prime opportunity. He explained later why Parks was such a perfect candidate for testing the law: "She was decent. And she was committed. First off, nobody could point no dirt at her. You had to respect her as a lady. And second, if she said she would be at a certain place at a certain time, that's when she got there. . . . So when she stood up to talk, people'd shut up and listen. And when she did something, people just figured it was the right thing to do." Ray Parks was afraid that segregationist whites might try to hurt Parks for daring to bring a lawsuit against segregated bus seating, but she was adamant in her desire to test the law. Still, she recognized that the likelihood of her receiving justice in the Alabama judicial system was slim.

Rosa Parks's case was not the first time an opportunity to challenge the system had presented itself. Several months earlier, another black woman, 15-year-old Claudette Colvin, had also been arrested for refusing to yield her seat to a white passenger. Claudette had been seated in the filled black section of the bus, but when the seats in the front of the bus were

IN HER OWN WORDS...

In an interview with the Academy of Achievement some four decades after her civil rights milestone, Rosa Parks reflected on the unforgettable Thursday, December 1, 1955:

Back in Montgomery during my growing up there, it was completely legally enforced racial segregation, and of course, I struggled against it for a long time. I felt that it was not right to be deprived of freedom when we were living in the Home of the Brave and Land of the Free.

Of course, when I refused to stand up on the orders of the bus driver, for a white passenger to take the seat, and I was not sitting in the front of the bus, as many people have said, and neither was my feet hurting as many people have said. But . . . I made up my mind that I would not give in any longer to legally imposed racial segregation . . . and of course my arrest brought about the protests for more than a year.

And in doing so, Dr. Martin Luther King became prominent because he was the leader of our protests along with many other people. And I'm very glad that this experience I had then brought about a movement that triggered across the United States and in other places.

Though the Thirteenth Amendment outlawed slavery in 1865, slavery in the form of segregation and discrimination continued in the South for decades. These passengers sit on a segregated trolley in Atlanta in 1956.

completely occupied, the driver asked the first row of blacks to give up their seats and stand. Claudette stayed where she was, and no white took the vacant seat next to her. The bus driver grew so angry he drove into town without stopping and called for a street policeman to arrest Claudette. When she refused to get up, two policemen dragged her, kicking and screaming hysterically, off the bus, and she was later tried and convicted for violating state segregation statutes, as well as for resisting arrest, disorderly conduct, and assault and battery. Many people regarded the convictions as an injustice, but because Claudette was pregnant and unmarried at the time, she was not regarded as an especially sympathetic public figure, and some blacks feared that she would reflect unfavorably on the black community.

But there was nothing that could be said to impugn the morality and respectability of Rosa Parks, and it was immediately recognized that she was an ideal figure behind whom to mount a nonviolent challenge to the centuries-old system of legal racial oppression in the South. What neither she nor anyone else could have foreseen was that the spontaneous individual action of this self-described "timid" woman would give rise to a collective movement that would force the entire United States, not just the city government of Montgomery, to confront its legacy of racial inequality and its professed belief in Thomas Jefferson's words, from the Declaration of Independence, that all men are created equal.

No Ordinary Little Girl

Rosa Parks was born Rosa McCauley on February 4, 1913, in Tuskegee, Alabama, 45 miles east of Montgomery. She was the first child of James and Leona McCauley, who named her after her maternal grandmother, Rose. Rosa was a tiny baby prone to sickness, and chronic tonsillitis plagued her throughout her childhood. Her mother felt lonely and ill equipped to raise a child. In her autobiography, *Rosa Park: My Story*, Rosa speculates about her mother's sadness, "I guess she was unhappy because my father worked on building homes in different places in the country and she was left alone."

James McCauley was a carpenter from Abbeville, Alabama. Skilled in brick and stone masonry, he spent most of his time away from home, building houses. Rosa's mother, Leona Edwards, was an elementary school teacher from Pine Level, Alabama. She was one of three daughters, and her father had insisted that she be educated so she would not have to work as a domestic, cooking and cleaning for white people. Leona had attended Payne University in Selma, Alabama, where she had earned a teaching certificate. When she returned home to teach at the black school in Pine Level, she met James McCauley at the Mt. Zion African Methodist Episcopal Church, where his brother was serving as pastor. In April 1912, when they were both 24, James and Leona were married at the Mt. Zion Church and went to live in Tuskegee, where James had some building contracts and Leona soon took a teaching job.

Tuskegee is home to the famous Tuskegee Institute, a school for blacks founded by Booker T. Washington in 1881. James's brother Robert joined the household briefly while attending building courses at Tuskegee, but Robert, an experienced carpenter, soon found himself providing key information to the teachers. Student life had not yielded anything new, so he returned to practicing construction.

Leona wanted to stay in Tuskegee and have James take a job teaching building courses at the institute, but James soon moved the family to his parents' home in Abbeville. Shortly afterward, he left Rosa and Leona with his parents to go north and build houses. Leona was pregnant with Rosa's younger brother Sylvester, who was born a year after Rosa, and she decided to take Rosa with her and return to her parents' home in Pine Level. Though James later joined the family in Pine Level, he did not stay long. When Rosa was just two and a half, James left again. He returned for a few days when Rosa was five and sometimes sent the family money through the mail, but Rosa did not see her father again throughout her childhood.

UP FROM SLAVERY

Rosa and Sylvester were raised by their mother and their maternal grandparents in a small house on the 18-acre Edwards family farm in Pine Level. The little house and six acres of land had been given to Rosa's grandmother Rose by a white girl she had cared for on the neighboring Hudson

Rosa Parks was born on February 4, 1913 to Leona and James McCauley. Leona, seen here (seated) with her cousin Beatrice, had a teaching certificate from Payne University, and raised Rosa in Pine Level, Alabama, where she taught elementary school.

plantation. The gift augmented the Edwardses' existing 12 acres and gave Rosa's grandparents—former slaves on the Hudson plantation—a place of their own to live.

Grandma Rose often told Rosa stories of what life had been like during the Civil War. Rosa's grandmother was just a young child during the war, but she remembered how the masters had made their slaves bury all the household valuables—jewelry, silver, and dishes—so the Yankee soldiers would not steal or destroy them when they marched through the area. The slave children were then sent out to play on the freshly dug soil to mat it down and disguise evidence of digging. After the war, like many of the freed slaves, Grandma Rose's family had stayed on the plantation. Grandma Rose herself was only six years old when she began caring for a little white girl on the plantation.

Rosa's grandfather Sylvester was the son of a white plantation overseer and a black house slave. His parents had died soon after he was born, and the new overseer had hated Sylvester so much that he had beaten and starved him. He told Rosa the story of how the overseer once beat him so badly he could not walk without a limp. After emancipation, Rosa's grandparents purchased 12 acres of land that had belonged to the Hudsons, and they continued to work on the plantation for wages. Like many freed slaves, they had no other place to go and did not want to leave the only home they had known. Even so, Rosa's grandfather held an intense hatred toward white people. He angered whites with his familiarity toward them and his practice of introducing himself to them by his last name. Blacks were only supposed to use their first name when speaking to whites. Rosa remembered, "It was my grandfather who instilled in my mother and her sisters and in their children that you don't put up with bad treatment from anybody. It was passed down almost in our genes." Her grandfather discouraged Rosa and her brother from playing with white children on the plantation and yelled at them if they even talked to the white girls and boys.

PLANTING FREEDOM

Rosa's grandparents kept a garden, raised chickens and a few cows, and harvested the fruit, pecan, and walnut trees that abounded on their land. Rosa grew up working alongside her mother and grandparents on the farm and looking after her baby brother. Besides farming their own land, Rosa's family picked peanuts, sweet potatoes, corn, and cotton for the Hudson plantation. Rosa started picking cotton when she was six years old, this was the typical age slave children were fully employed by their owners, working beside her grandparents at a rate of one dollar for every 100 pounds picked. When she was older, Rosa began chopping cotton for 50 cents a day under the hot Alabama sun; she never forgot how the soil burned into her feet even when she wore work shoes.

Though Rosa's family was poor, they managed to grow or raise almost everything they needed at home. Rosa's grandfather traded eggs for other supplies at the local store and sold some of the chickens and calves they raised. Rosa's mother sewed clothes for the entire family with cloth obtained in trade at the store. Because there was no doctor's office in Pine Level, Rosa would see the doctor at the town store. One of her earliest memories was of going to the store with her grandfather to have the doctor look at her throat. He set her right on the countertop and checked her tonsils. All the people in the store were very impressed with how well-behaved the little girl was and how nicely she obeyed the doctor's orders.

IN HER OWN WORDS...

Rosa Parks explains in her autobiography:

By the time I was six, I was old enough to realize that we were not actually free. Ku Klux Klan was riding through the black community, burning churches, beating up people, killing people. At the time I didn't realize why there was so much Klan activity, but later I learned that it was because African-American soldiers were returning from World War I and acting as if they deserved equal rights because they had served their country.

Although Rosa's mother was a schoolteacher, the scarcity of black schools in the area sometimes made it difficult for her to get a teaching position, so she earned money by doing hairdressing for neighbors and sewing for other black families. Rosa's training as a seamstress began at her mother's knee. Rosa said that despite their poverty, her "family tried to instill in me that we should all be equal, whether we had the money or the material goods, that we could be respected and respect other people." Rosa remembered hearing her family talk about the time that a white man treated her as if she were a little white girl, not a little black girl. "It was right after World War I, around 1919. I was five or six years old. Moses Hudson, the owner of the plantation next to our land in Pine Level, came out from the city of Montgomery to visit and stopped by the house. Moses had his son-in-law with him, a soldier from the North. They stopped in to visit my family. The Yankee soldier patted me on the head and said I was such a cute little girl." The soldier had treated Rosa as though she were as good and as pretty as any other little girl, something that a white southerner would have been unlikely to do in Alabama in 1919.

EDUCATION SEPARATE AND UNEQUAL

In the autumn after Rosa turned six, she began attending school in Pine Level. Sylvester, her brother, joined her the following year. The schoolhouse for black children was a dilapidated, old, one-room wooden-frame building that housed almost 60 students in grades one through six. (As was true of every other aspect of public life in Alabama and elsewhere in the South, public education was segregated under the law. At that time, the state and county did not even provide public funds for the education of its black citizens.) Inside the black schoolhouse, the students sat crowded on benches in rows according to their age. Rosa sat on a bench with the other six-year-olds. Because Rosa was so small for her age, her mother had waited until she was six to put her in school, but she was still so tiny that some of the other students teased her. There was just one teacher for all the students, who took turns standing up to read or recite. In winter, a wood stove heated the schoolroom, and the biggest boys carried in the firewood. Rosa, who had been taught by her mother, was already an avid reader by the time she started school, but Pine Level School did not have many books. Nor did it have any desks or windows.

On her way to school, which was only a short walk from home, Rosa had to pass by the new brick school for white children in the center of town. The white school had a play-ground and was financed with public money from taxes paid by both blacks and whites. White students rode to school on a bus, but black children had to walk. Sometimes when Rosa and Sylvester were walking to school, the buses passed them on the road, and the white kids threw trash and papers out the windows at them. The two McCauley children learned to veer away from the road when the school buses approached so they would not get hit.

Though many white schools in the South were open for nine months each year, most black schools only held classes for five or six months, since so many of their students were the children of sharecroppers and were needed to help out with the plowing and planting in the spring and the harvest-ing in the fall. (Unlike the Edwardses, most blacks in the rural South did not own their own land. Most of them worked a portion of land for the owner in exchange for a share of the crops.) After school let out in the afternoon, Rosa and the other students would take all of their books and belongings home with them, unable to leave anything behind because of the constant possibility that the Ku Klux Klan might burn down the school overnight.

Many nights, Rosa lay in bed unable to sleep for fear that white-robed Klansmen, on one of their nocturnal missions of terror, would ride to her family's house and kill her and all of

Ku Klux Klan

Groups of white men that slaves often called "paddyrollers" served as the outside enforcement arm for slaveholders. While denying any connection to theses provocateurs, "paddyrollers" could be dispatched to capture wayward slaves, physically intimidate both slaves and free persons of color, or exact the ultimate punishment in the form of a horrifying death.

With the demise of slavery at the end of the Civil War, the threat of a new and decidedly colorful power structure triggered some Southern land barons and businessmen to protect their wealthy status by relying on violence and intimidation similar to the "paddyrollers" of yesteryear. The Ku Klux Klan was one such organization, established in May 1866 by members of the former Confederate Army. It originated with its first Grand Wizard, former Confederate General Nathan Forrest, in a period of time when the South lived under Union military rule and a start was made to give black men equal rights in law as well as practice. Blacks were a political majority in many southern states and, in some minds, required tight control.

In Pulaski, within the King Cotton state of Tennessee, the Confederates came together supposedly for social purposes. They were a fraternal order of white businessmen, politicians, and workers, and indeed a Klansman could be the sheriff, mayor, or banker. From another perspective, that fraternal order was dedicated to keeping blacks on the lowest rungs of the political and economic ladders. Marauding Klansmen threatened blacks, who tried to leave plantations and strike out on their own. Their brutality impacted the 1866 elections and grew more organized at shutting out the newly granted black vote. The Klan and other similar white supremacists so terrorized black communities that a law was passed to stem their terrorism. This 1871 act, like the other civil rights laws of its time, was not sufficiently enforced and only a few states created black militias to counteract the violence.

Mayhem by white supremacists continued to reach heightened proportions following World War I. Klan membership ranged from four to five million across the nation during the 1920s. It is safe to say that most black men, women, and children were schooled on ways to avoid or at least survive their attacks. Still, thousand of African Americans lost their lives. The Ku Klux Klan continued to terrorize blacks throughout the mid twentieth century, and members of this white supremacist group still exist in the United States, although their activities were curtailed in the 1980s by a series of lawsuits won on behalf of victims by the Southern Poverty Law Office.

her relatives. "I had grown up in a community through which the Ku Klux Klan would ride periodically," she later wrote. "My grandfather kept his double-barreled shotgun handy at all times to protect our home and our lives. I believe the chronic insomnia I developed later was because as a child, whenever the Klan was riding, I could not sleep." The Ku Klux Klan was especially active during Rosa's childhood because of the return of many black soldiers who had served in the U.S. military during World War I. Having fought for their country and sampled greater freedom in Europe, these men were less willing than they might previously have been to accept the various segregational restraints on their freedom, and the Klan was determined to terrorize them into submission.

EDUCATION STILL A PRIZE

Rosa spent only a short time at the Pine Level School, which shut down not long after she started there. After a summer spent with an aunt in Montgomery, where her mother, Leona, renewed her teaching certificate at Alabama State Normal, a black teachers' college, Rosa and her brother resumed their education at the Spring Hill Church School. Leona, who took a teaching job at the school, boarded with a family who lived nearby, but Rosa and her brother walked the eight miles to classes every day. One day, Rosa encountered a white boy named Franklin on her way to school. The youth called her names, balled up his hand into a fist, and threatened to hit her, so Rosa picked up a brick to defend herself, and the bully backed off. When Rosa told her grandmother about the incident, she said Rosa should not have retaliated. If she did not stop being so high-strung around whites, Grandmother McCauley said, she was likely to be lynched before she was 21.

At age 11, Rosa graduated from the sixth and final grade of the Spring Hill Church School, and her mother decided to send her to private school in Montgomery. Although this meant a considerable financial sacrifice for the family, Leona

McCauley felt that she had little choice, as there were no public high schools in the area. So when Rosa's mother had saved enough money to pay her tuition, Rosa was enrolled at the Montgomery Industrial School for Black Girls, known as Miss White's School. The principal and cofounder Alice L. White was a transplanted New Englander who was ostracized by fellow European Americans in Montgomery because she operated a school for blacks. The school had an enrollment of 250 girls, who were taught academic subjects as well as the skills of sewing, cooking, rug making, and basket weaving. Leona sent Rosa to live with her sister, Fannie Williamson, and five cousins in Montgomery for the school year.

All of Rosa's teachers at Miss White's School were white women from the North, which also made them pariahs in Montgomery's white community. The teachers socialized with the black community and attended all-black churches; twice, angry whites set fire to the school. Rosa excelled at school in Montgomery. Besides studying crafts and subjects like English, geography, and science, she learned domestic science—how to care for sick people and invalids in the home. At first, her mother paid Rosa's entire tuition, but when Leona could no longer afford it, Rosa became a scholarship student who cleaned blackboards, dusted desks, and swept floors in exchange for her tuition.

RACISM, A PECULIAR AND DANGEROUS INSTITUTION

Along with academic subjects, Rosa inevitably learned further lessons about the South's system of white supremacy. In good weather, Rosa walked from her Aunt Fannie's house to school, but if it rained, she rode the streetcars. The trolleys were segregated, and Rosa had to sit as far to the back as she could. All of Rosa's cousins went to public school, but they would meet Rosa and walk home from school with her in the after-noons. One day, Rosa and her cousin Annie Mae Williamson stopped at a five-and-dime store. When Annie asked the white woman behind the lunch counter for a soda, the woman said in reply, "I'll sell you an ice-cream cone." Annie did not understand what the woman meant and asked for a soda again. Eventually, the saleswoman leaned over the counter and whispered, "We don't sell sodas to colored people." Annie and Rosa left the store.

To get home after school, Rosa and her cousins had to walk through an all-white neighborhood, where, one day, a white boy on roller skates came up behind Rosa and tried to push her off the sidewalk. Rosa responded by pushing him back. "Why did you put your hands on my child?" the boy's mother said when she saw this. "Because he pushed me," Rosa replied. She remembered later that the woman told her "she could put me so far in jail I would never get out for pushing her child. So I told her that he had pushed me and that I didn't want to be pushed, seeing as how I wasn't bothering him at all." This incident was the most threatening of all of Rosa's encounters with whites so far. Most of the time, white children only made threats, and then Rosa and her cousins would talk rough to them to prevent further violence.

Once, while Rosa and Annie Mae were picking berries in a vacant lot adjacent to the white country club where Aunt Fannie worked as a maid, a little white boy yelled to them, "You niggers better leave them berries alone!" Rosa and Annie Mae yelled back, "If you come over here, we're going to give you a good beating!" and the boy ran away. When Aunt Fannie heard about this, she scolded Rosa and Annie Mae and told them that they could have been lynched for such insolence. This type of incident bred confusion in the mind of the young girl, who had difficulty understanding why adults gave her such advice; it seemed to Rosa that they should take her side. Even though they were only concerned for her safety, it seemed to Rosa that her family members were siding with the whites who had provoked her. Living in Montgomery exposed Rosa to blatant inequality, but attending Miss White's School taught her dignity and self-respect. She learned to have ambitions and to think that she could do what she wanted in life. As her mother and grandparents had brought her up, the teachers at Miss White's School taught her not to set her sights lower than anyone else's because she was black. This was a lesson Rosa remembered for the rest of her life.

At the end of Rosa's eighth-grade year, the school closed. It had not been able to recruit new teachers, and Miss White was now an elderly woman. Fortunately for Rosa, a black junior high school had just opened in Montgomery, and she was able to attend ninth grade at Booker T. Washington Junior High. Sylvester joined Rosa in Montgomery so he could go to the public school as well. One day, Rosa and Annie and Sylvester were gathering firewood for Aunt Fannie in the woods behind her house when a group of white boys approached them and threatened to throw Sylvester into the nearby creek. "You won't be throwing nobody in the creek unless all of us go in together!" Annie and Rosa retorted, and the boys backed down. Some time later, a group of white boys, possibly the same ones, came upon Sylvester and one of his friends in the woods. They began throwing rocks at 13-year-old Sylvester, and he and his friend started to throw rocks back. One of the white boys was hit and suddenly the white gang disappeared, only to return quickly with a man. The man had a pistol with him and was the father of one of the boys. He asked his son if Sylvester and his friend were the ones who had been throwing rocks at them. Surprisingly, the boy said no, these were not the same boys, and the whites left. Sylvester did not tell anyone about this close call until many years later when he was a grown man.

Rosa and her brother experienced much more discrimination and conflict in Montgomery than they had ever known with their grandparents in Pine Level. Pine Level had been too small to be very segregated, but in Montgomery all public

Because there were no public high schools for blacks in her neighborhood, Parks attended a private girls' school in Montgomery, Alabama. In Montgomery, Parks experienced more discrimination than before and found segregation everywhere from trolleys to water fountains to movie theaters.

facilities were segregated. When she first came to Aunt Fannie's house, Rosa wondered whether the water from the "whites" fountain tasted different from the water from the "coloreds" fountain. She soon realized that the only difference between the two facilities was the one invented by white people about who got to use which.

When Rosa graduated from junior high, there was still no public high school for blacks in Montgomery, so she attended 10th and 11th grades at the laboratory school of Alabama State College for Negroes. To help pay for her tuition, Rosa sometimes cleaned houses and did sewing for whites in Montgomery.

During her second month in 11th grade, however, Grandma Rose became ill and Rosa had to leave school to go home to take care of her. A month later, Grandma Rose died. Rosa was 16. She returned to Montgomery and got a job at a shirt factory, making men's blue denim work shirts. She attempted to resume her high school education at Alabama State, but when her mother became sick, Rosa had to quit school once again to return home to care for her. Fifteen-year-old Sylvester also left school and went to work as a carpenter to help pay the bills.

After her mother's condition improved, Rosa started doing occasional domestic work, but most of her time was spent running the family farm and looking after her mother, brother, and grandfather at home. Her childhood had been brief, and now the people who had raised her needed her to take care of them. Expectations and demands were placed on her at an early age, and Rosa worked hard to fulfill them.

3

Getting Involved

Following the stock market crash of 1929, the U.S. economy collapsed, leading to more than a decade of economic hard times known as the Great Depression. Between 1929 and 1933, the nation's gross national product shrank in half, banks failed across the country, and many American families lost their life savings. Poor rural areas, such as Pine Level, were among the hardest hit. Millions of jobless men and women and homeless families drifted from place to place, tramping the dusty southern roads or riding the rails atop trains in their search for work.

The McCauleys were fortunate to own their own house and land, for many tenant farmers and sharecropping families lost their homes and claims to land during the Great Depression. When the depression's effects began to be felt in rural Alabama, Rosa was a slender, soft-spoken young woman in her late teens who wore her hair up in tight pigtails across her head or wrapped up in two braids like a crown. Though still petite, she was a tireless worker who helped keep up the family farm and labored as a domestic servant in order to support her grandfather, mother, and brother.

A PERSISTENT SUITOR

In the spring of 1931, a friend of Rosa's introduced her to Raymond Parks, who was then 28 and worked as a barber at a black barbershop in downtown Montgomery. After they had been introduced, Ray tried to call on Rosa, but she was not especially interested in him and did not care to see him again. Despite such discouragements—once, upon learning that it was him at the door, Rosa ran upstairs and hid under the covers—Raymond began to make the drive regularly from Montgomery to the McCauley home in Pine Level in his flashy red Nash rambler with the rumble seat. His persistence wore Rosa down, and as they became better acquainted, first over conversation in the McCauley living room and then through longer discussions as they cruised the countryside in Ray's automobile, Rosa found much to admire in her suitor.

Raymond Parks, or Parks, as everyone, including Rosa, called him, was born in Wedowee, Alabama, on February 12, 1903. Like Rosa's father, Ray's father was a carpenter, a white man who took little responsibility for the son and daughter he had fathered. Ray was a baby when he had his last contact with his father; he eventually heard that his father had died after falling off a roof. Raised by his mother and grandmother, Ray was the only black child in the neighborhood where he grew up. With his father's blond hair, blue eyes, and pale skin, he actually looked white—one reason for Rosa's initial reluctance to date him was that she was not attracted to light-skinned black men—but he was still not allowed to attend the all-white school in Wedowee. Instead, his mother taught him at home.

After Ray's mother and grandmother died when he was in his late teens, his stepfather turned him and his younger sister

One early civil rights debate occurred in 1931 when nine black teenagers, called the "Scottsboro Boys," were wrongfully convicted of rape and sentenced to death. Here, marchers gather outside the White House in Washington, D.C., asking President Roosevelt to pardon the boys.

out of the family home. At first, Ray earned a living and supported his sister by working as a sexton, or caretaker, at a white Baptist church in Roanoke, Alabama, but that job came to an end after he had an argument with his white employers, and he decided to leave Roanoke. After arranging for a cousin to take in his baby sister, he rambled around the state in search of work, ending up finally in Tuskegee, Alabama, where he learned to cut and style men's hair.

Besides her grandfather Sylvester McCauley, Ray Parks was the first man with whom Rosa had ever frankly discussed civil rights. Like Rosa's grandfather, he "believed in being a man and expected to be treated like a man," as Rosa wrote in her autobiography, *Rosa Parks: My Story*, and he exhibited none of the meek, so-called Uncle Tom attitude that southern whites expected. A long-time member of the NAACP, he was not afraid of whites, and he was the first civil rights activist that Rosa had ever known. When Rosa met him, he was active in raising funds to help the cause of the Scottsboro Boys, nine black teenagers who had been falsely convicted of rape in 1931.

SETTLING IN AS A COUPLE

Ray Parks mentioned marriage the second time he went out with Rosa, but she took a while longer to be convinced. One day in August 1932, as they were talking, he suddenly blurted out, "I really think we ought to get married." By this time, Rosa had come to admire Ray for his activism and his courage, and she agreed. The next day, while Rosa was at church, he asked Leona McCauley for permission to marry her, and their engagement was set.

Ray and Rosa were married in December 1932, almost two years after they had first met. The ceremony, which took place at Rosa's family home in Pine Level, was a small, almost humble affair. No invitations were sent out, and only family members and close friends attended. After the wedding, the couple lived in a rooming house on South Jackson Street, on the east side of Montgomery, not far from Alabama State College. Both of them thought it was a good idea for Rosa to finish her high school education, so with Ray's support she went back to Alabama State Teacher's College. She received her high school diploma in 1933, at the age of 20.

As very few blacks in Alabama had completed a high school education, Rosa Parks was considered very well educated, but her diploma did not help her find a better job. Few blacks owned their own businesses, and most whites would not hire blacks for any position that required much academic proficiency. Regardless of their education, blacks generally were able only to obtain work doing what whites did not want to do: cleaning, cooking, sewing, babysitting, and domestic jobs as well as sanitation work, such as garbage collection and sewer

NAACP

Soon after the sun rose on a new century, W.E.B. Du Bois, William Monroe Trotter and twenty-seven other blacks met in Niagara Falls, New York. The group convened to outline a militant fight against the noose of American racism. It was 1905 and not much had changed for black people since emancipation. Contrary to the patience shown by Booker T. Washington, this group of young militants wanted to experience freedom now and raised their voices to that effect.

The Niagara Movement faltered as an organization due to spotty finances even while racial violence raged into the bloody riots of 1908. When a white mob stormed a black neighborhood in Springfield, Illinois, southern writer William English Walling grew anxious about a race war in the North. He, along with *New York Evening Post* reporter Mary White Orvington, and New York social worker Dr. Henry Moskovitz, also white, called for an organized and peaceful struggle against racial oppression. On February 12, 1909, Ida B. Wells, W.E.B. Du Bois, Oswald Garrison Villiard, William English Walling, and Mary White Ovington responded to the call with the National Negro Committee that in 1910 incorporated as the National Association for the Advancement of Colored People (NAACP).

Some fifty branches of the biracial organization extended throughout the country with the bulk of the membership by 1914 living in the South. In those early years they waged a battle against lynchings and lobbied Congress to pass an anti-lynching bill. They first entered the courtroom in the Pink Franklin case, involving a black farmhand who, in self-defense, killed the policeman who had broken into his house at 3:00 A.M. to arrest him on a civil charge. From that humble beginning the NAACP Legal Defense and Educational Fund emerged to batter down the *Plessy* v. *Ferguson* separate-but-equal ruling in an all out attack against segregation. *Brown* v. *Board of Education* caused legalized segregation to crumble in 1954, and *Gayle* v. *Browder*, the Montgomery bus transport class action suit, completely razed Jim Crow laws in public accommodations in 1956.

maintenance, and other menial positions. After her graduation, Rosa took a low-paying job as a helper at St. Margaret's Hospital in Montgomery; she supplemented the family's income by taking in sewing at home.

In 1941, Rosa took a job at Maxwell Field, an Army Air Force base. Although the armed forces themselves were still segregated (Sylvester McCauley, who would see service in the European and Pacific theaters of war during World War II, had been drafted the year before), blacks and whites shared the same facilities at Maxwell Field, which had been integrated by virtue of an order issued by President Franklin D. Roosevelt mandating desegregation at all U.S. military bases. Ray also obtained a job on the base, as a barber, and Rosa rode on integrated trolleys. But the instant she stepped off the base to go home, it was back to the old segregated system, and she had to ride in the rear of the city buses. A white woman who lived in the same boardinghouse as Ray and Rosa also worked on the base. Rosa often sat across from her on the base trolley, but when they left Maxwell Field to board a city bus for home in the evenings, the white woman would sit down in the front while Rosa walked all the way to the back. The woman's little boy, who often traveled to work with his mother, looked at Rosa at these times as if she were crazy, unable to understand why his mother's friend always walked all the way to the back of the bus when there were seats up front.

In a city as thoroughly segregated as Montgomery, there was no way for Rosa Parks (or any other black person) to escape the effects of legal discrimination, but this did not mean that she accepted those rules. A black person defied the Jim Crow laws only at great personal peril, but Parks found ways to silently protest the unjust laws by avoiding segregated facilities. She climbed the stairs instead of riding in a "colored" elevator. She went thirsty rather than drink from a "colored" public fountain. When she worked in Montgomery, she walked home from work whenever bus drivers forced her to enter

Both Parks and her husband belonged to the NAACP, whose members are seen finding new volunteers at this New York City sidewalk recruiting station. The organization, founded in 1909, was dedicated to ending inequality and segregation and worked to achieve this through education and defending blacks in legal battles.

their vehicle through the back door. Those drivers who required blacks to enter from the rear sometimes recognized the bespectacled Parks and would tell her that if she "was too important to go to the back door, she should stay off the bus." But Rosa was not resigned to segregation; although at that time she did not yet belong to any civil rights organizations, she wanted to improve conditions for blacks and was willing to work hard toward that goal.

Though Ray Parks was a member of the NAACP, he initially felt that it might be too dangerous for Rosa to join the organization. (The meetings he attended in support of the Scottsboro

Boys, for example, had to be conducted at night, in secret, at constantly shifting locations, often with the participants armed, for fear of detection by white vigilantes or the police.) Founded on February 12, 1909, the centennial of Abraham Lincoln's birthday, the NAACP was a multiracial organization dedicated to the goal of ending racial inequality and segregation. In the 1930s, most of its efforts toward that end were still devoted to halting lynching; in the next decade, the NAACP would focus on attaining equal rights in education as the best way for future generations of black Americans to achieve equal opportunity.

Rosa was not even aware that the Montgomery branch of the NAACP had any female members until she saw a picture in the *Alabama Tribune* of Johnnie Carr, one of her old friends from Miss White's School, who was then the local chapter's acting secretary. Bolstered by her friend's membership, Rosa decided to attend the annual Montgomery NAACP meeting for the election of officers in 1943, only to find herself the lone female among the 16 individuals present. As the post of secretary was considered a woman's position, Rosa found herself elected to the office by default; she was too timid, she said, to say no.

Rosa Parks began by taking minutes at that very meeting and stayed on in the volunteer position for the next 12 years. She arranged meetings, notified members about current events, sent letters, kept minutes at every meeting, recorded and sent membership payments to the national office, answered phones, wrote letters, and issued press releases. The work was demanding, but she thrived on it. It gave her an opportunity to use her education and channel her energy toward a cause to which she was truly dedicated.

4

The New Order

One of Rosa Parks's most important jobs for the NAACP was helping the chapter's president, E.D. Nixon, document every case of racial discrimination and violence against blacks that occurred in Alabama. Among the hundreds of cases she recorded was that of Recy Taylor from Abbeville, Alabama, Parks's father's hometown. Taylor had been walking home alone from church one Sunday when a car filled with white men pulled over next to her. The men forced her into the car at gun- and knife-point, and all six tore off her clothes and took turns raping her. Even though the driver of the car confessed to the crime and named his accomplices, a grand jury appointed to hear the case declared that the men were innocent. An inter-racial citizens' committee was formed to help Taylor, and this group contacted the Montgomery NAACP for assistance. Although the NAACP was able to get the governor to convene a special grand jury to review the case, this jury refused to indict the white men.

Taylor's case illustrated one of the greatest difficulties the NAACP had to overcome: all-white southern juries simply would not convict whites of violence against blacks. But if whites charged blacks with an offense, juries would convict them on the flimsiest evidence. Such was the case with the Scottsboro Boys, who were falsely accused of rape by two white women, convicted by all-white juries, and sentenced to death.

One of the biggest difficulties Parks experienced in working on such cases was getting black witnesses to come forward to testify against whites. "I happened to be the secretary of the Montgomery branch of the NAACP as well as the NAACP Youth Council adviser," Parks began her explanation about previous bus incidences for the oral history *Voices of Freedom*. "Many cases did come to my attention that nothing came out of 'cause the person that was abused would be too intimidated to sign an affidavit or to make a statement."

Black witnesses feared reprisals against themselves, their homes, and their families if they dared to accuse a white person of a crime. Once Parks tried to take a statement for the NAACP from a black minister who had run 15 miles to Montgomery to report a murder. The minister had witnessed a white man killing a black man, but when Parks tried to write up the report, he became too frightened for his own safety and could not go through with it. Unfortunately, without notarized statements from witnesses, and without plaintiffs to press charges, the NAACP did not have enough evidence to present in a court of law when the time came for legal action.

IMMERSED IN THE MOVEMENT

After Nixon stepped down as NAACP branch president, Parks continued to work with him as his personal secretary on civil rights issues. Through her work as secretary of the Alabama State conference of NAACP branches, she had met many

Scottsboro Boys

Justice took a vacation during the case of the Scottsboro nine in 1931. Nine itinerant blacks, Charley Weems, Ozzie Powell, Clarence Norris, Olen Montgomery, and Willie Roberson from Georgia, and Haywood Patterson, Eugene Williams, and brothers Andrew and LeRoy Wright, from the ages of twelve to twenty hopped a freight train in Chattanooga, Tennessee, bound for Memphis. A scuffle ensued with some white boys also riding the Depression rails. The whites, after being tossed off the train, reported the incident to the stationmaster who relayed it to Jackson County sheriffs in Alabama, where the train would pass.

When the train was stopped by authorities in Paint Rock, Alabama, the black boys were arrested for vagrancy and inciting a riot. But two white girls dressed in men's attire, Nancy Bates and Victoria Price, were also found in a corner of the same freight car. Being in close proximity to blacks presented a difficult situation for these girls, who were rumored to be prostitutes. After considerable discussions with the police, the girls claimed rape.

Taken to Scottsboro for trial on the harsher crime of rape, eight of the boys were found guilty by an all-white jury and sentenced to death. A mistrial was declared for one of the youngest defendants, LeRoy Wright. His case was eventually remanded to juvenile court by a different judge. Williams, the other thirteen-year-old, was granted a new trial.

The eyes of the world were watching the Communist Party and NAACP help during the appeals to the U.S. Supreme Court, which twice overturned the convictions of the remaining seven. These rulings remain critical to justice today because they established the precedent for guaranteeing the right of the accused to appropriate counsel in state level trials and disallowed the exclusion of Negroes from jury lists in concert with the Fourteenth Amendment.

The first ruling afforded the remaining seven young men second trials in which they were convicted again even though there had been no physical evidence of rape and Nancy Bates recanted her story at Patterson's first of three retrials. "I'd rather die than spend my life in jail for something I didn't do," declared Patterson to Roy Wilkins of the NAACP and his white attorney Clarence Watts about a possible sentence reduction to seventy-five years in prison. He managed to escape in 1948, but wound up in a Michigan prison where he remained the rest of his life.

The second Supreme Court reversal led to charges being dropped for four of the original nine men–Montgomery, Roberson, and the youngest two, Eugene Williams and LeRoy Wright. Powell pled guilty to assaulting a deputy. The rest, including Patterson, were retried and convicted in 1936 and 1937. Three of them were subsequently paroled. The last one, Andy Wright, gained release in 1950.

leading civil rights activists, including Ella Baker, A. Philip Randolph, and Roy Wilkins, national president of the NAACP. In the evenings after she had left her work at a tailoring shop, Parks would often help out at Nixon's downtown office. (In addition to his work with the NAACP, Nixon was active in the Brotherhood of Sleeping Car Porters, a trade union founded by A. Philip Randolph that had long been in the forefront of civil rights issues; and he was head of the Progressive Democrats, a liberal political organization in Montgomery.) Rosa Parks, Nixon said, "is secretary for everything I have going."

Parks also worked as the secretary to the senior citizens' brigade of the NAACP and as adviser to the NAACP Youth Council. Parks's youth group of high school students met weekly in the Trinity Lutheran Church. One of their projects was organizing students to try to take books out of Montgomery's white library. The students would ask for a title that was not available at the black library, saying that they needed the book for a school report. When they were told they had to wait until it could be sent over from the white library, they would try to take the book out themselves. Although the students tried again and again, they were always refused access to books at the white library.

When the Freedom Train, an exhibition that included the original versions of the U.S. Constitution and the Bill of Rights, stopped in Montgomery as part of its nationwide tour, Parks decided to take her youth group to visit the historic exhibit, which was free and open to the public on an integrated basis. But after the students in her group attended the exhibit alongside groups of white children, Parks received threatening phone calls from whites who were angry that she had brought black children into the train while white children were there.

Parks also recruited young people for the United Negro College Fund, an organization that provided scholarships and financial aid to black college students. In this capacity, Parks did her best to connect bright students, not just from

Rosa Parks volunteered as secretary of the Montgomery branch of the NAACP for 12 years starting in 1943, and later became advisor of the NAACP Youth Council. Parks performed a variety of duties for the NAACP in a busy office like this while continuing her full-time job as a seamstress.

Montgomery but also from the rural South, with the organization. Parks would help these students prepare for an interview, dress respectably, and learn good personal habits. After she took a position as a tailor's assistant at the downtown Montgomery Fair department store, she often talked with her co-workers about the plight of young people she knew who needed money for college. Parks remembered how hard it was for her own family to earn money to send her to school in Montgomery, and how her education had been interrupted when her mother and grandmother had become ill. She also knew that without an education she would not have been able to do any of her civil rights work, so she wanted to do whatever she could to give young blacks the opportunity to go to school and learn. Although her marriage proved childless, it was often said of her that "she has no children but thinks of all children as her own."

THE POWER OF THE BALLOT

Another primary concern of the NAACP and similar civil rights organizations was the right of southern blacks to vote. Although the Fifteenth Amendment to the Constitution, ratified in 1870, declared that "the right of citizens of the United States to vote shall not be denied by the United States or by any state on account of race, color, or previous condition of servitude," white southerners used various methods, such as a poll tax (designed especially to keep blacks from being able to pay) and a literacy test (applied invariably in discriminatory fashion) to keep blacks from the polls. To rectify the situation, a group calling itself the Montgomery Voters League was formed in the 1940s and met frequently at the Parkses' home. When the league formed, there were only 31 names on the list of registered black voters in Montgomery, and most of those people had long since died.

To assist the Voters League in its work, Nixon enlisted Arthur Madison, a black attorney from Alabama then practicing law in New York City. Madison explained that, under the law, in order to register to vote blacks did not have to bring a white person who would vouch for their character with them to the registrar's office, a practice that white government officials in Montgomery had sought to impose. Blacks, however, would still have to pass a literacy test to prove that they could read, write, and understand the U.S. Constitution. While whites were generally asked to do nothing more than read a line or two of the Constitution aloud, blacks were made to pass a written examination consisting of 21 questions.

In addition, voter registration officials did everything in their power to make it extremely difficult for blacks to even attempt to register. They opened the registration books only at a certain time each day, without announcing in advance what that time would be. Blacks had to call to find out if the books were open; most often the registrars opened the books at the most inaccessible times, such as during the late morning or early afternoon, when most blacks would be at work.

When Parks first took the voter registration test in 1943, the registrar told her, "You should have property in order to register to vote, but if you can pass the test by answering these questions correctly, you don't have to have property." Despite her belief to the contrary, Parks was told that she had not passed the test. Madison, meanwhile, was arrested on trumped-up charges for his role in teaching Montgomery's blacks how to register, and he eventually returned to his practice in the North. She tried again, and again she thought she had passed, but the registrar told her that she had not. Parks disbelieved him.

The third year she took the test, she brought Nixon with her and copied down her answers to the 21 questions to use as evidence in a suit against the voter registration board, should she be told again that she had failed. This time, Parks received a certificate in the mail saying that she had passed. But not all of Montgomery's blacks were as persistent, resourceful, or educated enough to pass the literacy test, or secure enough economically to afford the poll tax. Parks was 32 when she finally became a registered voter in 1945; as applied retroactively for every year since she had become eligible to vote at age 21, the yearly poll tax of $1.50 had accumulated to $16.50 (equivalent to approximately $115 today)—an amount of money significant enough to discourage many prospective voters.

Though Parks and other members of the Montgomery Voters League continued to coach blacks on how to pass their registration exams and to encourage blacks to vote, progress was slow, and at times Parks grew frustrated by the reluctance of other blacks to stand up against injustice. On the occasion of her second attempt to register to vote, for example, she was thrown off a city bus when she refused to reenter it through the back door after she had already paid at the front. Even as she was exiting, she could hear the confused voices of blacks issuing from the back of the bus and asking, "How come she don't go around and get in the back? She ought to go around the back and get in." The failure of other blacks to understand her unwillingness to comply with discriminatory treatment frustrated her terribly.

A NEW DAY STUCK IN THE SAME OLD CLOTHES

But, over time, Parks and the thousands of others working for equality did see some rewards from their peaceful, patient protests. On May 17, 1954, the U.S. Supreme Court ruled unanimously in the case of *Brown* v. *the Board of Education of Topeka, Kansas,* which addressed five separate lawsuits filed by the NAACP, that the doctrine of "separate but equal" as it applied to public education was unconstitutional because "separate educational facilities are inherently unequal." In addition to providing black children with equal access to public education, the ruling—perhaps the most momentous in the history of the high court—sounded the death knell to almost a century of legalized segregation in the South.

While white southerners prepared to resist the new order that the *Brown* ruling heralded with individual violence, organized governmental defiance at the state and local level, and all manner of legal obfuscation, the NAACP and other organizations devised strategies to test the ruling's implications for the desegregation of other aspects of public life as well. The Alabama NAACP decided to use cases of arrests for violations of the state's Jim Crow laws to test the courts; although its lawyers knew they were unlikely to receive justice from all-white juries in local venues, their strategy was to appeal the guilty verdicts in the federal courts, where they had a better chance of being judged fairly and receiving protection under the law.

NAACP lawyers George Hayes, Thurgood Marshall, and James Nabrit celebrate outside the U.S. Supreme Court in Washington, D.C., after hearing the ruling in the case of *Brown* v. *Board of Education*. The NAACP and civil rights workers, like Parks, saw the first major reward for their work when the Supreme Court ruled in *Brown* that segregation was illegal.

In Montgomery, the likeliest sources of such a test case were the laws regulating segregated seating on the city's buses. As early as the mid-1940s, Montgomery's blacks had begun to organize in protest of the way Montgomery City Lines (the bus company that held the city charter) treated its black passengers, who constituted three-quarters of the line's riders. "The Women's Political Council had begun in 1946, after just dozens of black people had been arrested on buses for segregation purposes," explained Jo Ann Robinson for *Voices of Freedom*. She, a professor of English at Alabama State College, was mistreated aboard a city bus in 1949 when she failed to move to the vehicle's rear. "It was then," Robinson later said, "that I made up . . . my mind that whatever I could add to that organization [the Women's Political Council] that would help to bring that practice down, I would do it."

Upon bringing her complaints to the WPC, Robinson learned that many other black women had similar stories to tell; the organization estimated that three out of every five blacks in Montgomery had suffered abusive treatment on the city's public transportation. "Everyone would look the other way," she was quoted as saying by historian David Garrow in *Bearing the Cross*. "Nobody would acknowledge what was going on. It outraged me that this kind of conduct was going on and that so far no black community organizations had done anything about it."

Robinson's outrage would soon lead to her becoming the president of the WPC, which repeatedly petitioned the city government and Montgomery City Lines about segregated seating, the practice of making black passengers reboard buses through the rear door, the abusive attitude and behavior of the company's white drivers, and the fact that bus stops in black neighborhoods were spaced twice as far apart as they were in white neighborhoods. Though Parks agreed with most of the WPC's goals, she opposed its methods and was not a member. Petitions were not her way; with her grandfather's pride, she had resolved never to approach whites with a piece of paper in hand and ask for favors.

Meanwhile, incidents on Montgomery City Lines buses continued to multiply. In 1952, a black man named Brooks was accused of failing to put a dime in the slot when he boarded a bus; as he left the bus, he was shot and killed by city police, who claimed that he was resisting arrest. In 1953, Epsie Worthy boarded a city bus at a transfer point with a transfer, only to be ordered by the driver to pay the fare; when she exited, she was followed by the driver, who began to beat her. Her efforts at self-defense earned her an arrest and conviction for disorderly conduct. Geneva Johnson was arrested for disorderly conduct when she verbally protested a driver's insistence that she pay her fare with exact change; two visiting children from New Jersey, unfamiliar with legalized segregation, were arrested for sitting in the whites-only section of the bus.

In the wake of the *Brown* ruling, Nixon looked for a test case with which to challenge the city's segregation ordinances. Robinson had even begun to contemplate the potential effectiveness of a boycott of the city buses by Montgomery's black population, although the WPC leader was not yet sure that the sentiment of the community had been sufficiently outraged to support such an endeavor. Both leaders were only waiting for the right case, and for the right moment to put their plans into effect.

The WPC enlarged with its mind on one day acting against the bus system. "By 1955, we had members in every elementary, junior high, and senior high school, and in federal, state, and local jobs. Wherever there were more than ten blacks employed, we had a member there. We were prepared to the point that we knew that in a matter of hours, we could corral the whole city," Jo Ann Robinson told *Voices of Freedom*.

5

The Movement Organizes

On March 2, 1955, a 15-year-old honor student named Claudette Colvin was arrested and convicted under Alabama state law for refusing to yield her seat on a Montgomery bus to a white passenger. Rosa Parks was very excited about the Colvin case and spoke with Jo Ann Robinson and Nixon about its suitability as a test in the federal courts, but both leaders agreed that Colvin's resistance to her arrest and her pregnancy made her case somewhat problematic.

That summer, Parks participated in a workshop at the Highlander Folk School near Monteagle, Tennessee, in the Cumberland Plateau of the Appalachian Mountains in the south-central part of the state, not far from the Alabama border. This remarkable educational institution had been founded by a white man named Myles Horton in 1932 as a means of educating the poor inhabitants of the Appalachians in methods of dealing with the myriad economic and social problems of the region. Horton's educational philosophy rested on the belief that, as a group, economically and politically oppressed individuals—be they the poor white denizens of Appalachia or southern blacks—possessed all the knowledge necessary to solve their own problems. "They've got much of the knowledge as a group," Horton said in 1972 about his methods. "Not as individuals, but the group as a whole has much of the knowledge that they need to know to solve their problems. If they only knew how to analyze what their experiences were, what they know, and generalize them . . . they would begin to draw on their own resources." Horton and his colleagues at the school sought to train potential community leaders to make the necessary analyses; these leaders were then to return to their communities, where they would apply what they had learned. From the beginning, Horton had conceived of Highlander as a racially integrated institution, and in the 1950s Highlander began to focus on civil rights issues and race relations. Blacks and whites would meet there for two-week sessions to discuss national and local events, ways to overcome segregation, and means of organizing and leading protests. The school also conducted workshops in public speaking and literacy, designed to give blacks the knowledge they needed in order to register to vote.

Parks had learned about the Highlander School through Virginia Durr, to whom she had been introduced by Nixon the previous year. She and her husband Clifford, a lawyer, were two of the first whites dedicated to civil rights that Parks had ever met. Virginia Durr hired Parks as a seamstress for her children's clothes, including her daughter's wedding trousseau, and Parks became a frequent participant in an integrated women's prayer group that met at the Durr home until some white husbands broke it up. In the summer of 1955, Virginia Durr arranged for Parks to receive a scholarship at the Highlander Folk School for its workshop on "Racial Desegregation: Implementing the Supreme Court

Rosa Parks and other students attending class at the Highlander Folk School, an institution founded to educate the poor and underprivileged to deal with economic and social problems. Parks's time at the school in August 1955 encouraged her enthusiasm for her social causes.

Decision," and she paid for the cost of Parks's transportation to and from the school.

The 10 days that Parks spent at the Highlander Folk School at the end of August 1955 constituted one of the most important experiences of her life. It marked the first time she had ever been north of Alabama, and the rugged beauty of the land-scape took her breath away. More important, she completed the workshop with a heightened sense of self-confidence and commitment to social change. As he explained in a 1978 interview with historian Aldon Morris in *The Origins of the Civil Rights Movement*, Horton had always emphasized that change had to begin from below, with the people themselves. Blacks "couldn't wait for some government edict or some Messiah" to act against segregation, Horton taught; though southern whites bore the responsibility for the myriad injustices of Jim Crow, blacks had to assume the responsibility for changing the system. "Blacks would often say to me," Horton said, "'It isn't right that we have to struggle, we have to stick our necks out, that we have to take chances. We didn't ask for this. The people who are doing this to us should have to change, and they should be the ones that do this.'" Horton agreed, but he invariably pointed out that the "reality was [southern whites] are not going to change, the realities are they never will, and there's nothing in history to suggest that they will, so the right thing is not going to be done. . . . So if that's not going to be done, black people are going to have to force the white people to respect them. . . . The burden and the responsibility is on the whites, but the burden of change is on the blacks."

PREPARED FOR BATTLE

To at least one observer, the effect of Horton's teachings on Parks was immediately discernible. According to Septima Clark, the school's director of education, Parks was virtually transformed by her experience at Highlander, which exists today as Highlander Research and Education Center in New Market, Tennessee. Shy and somewhat withdrawn upon her arrival, uncertain whether she could trust the whites who were participating in the workshop, "Rosa Parks was afraid for white people to know that she was as militant as she was," Clark explained to Morris in 1978. "She didn't want to speak before the whites that she met up there [at Highlander], because she was afraid they would take it back to the whites in Montgomery. After she talked it out in that workshop that morning and she went back home, then she decided that 'I'm not going to move out of that seat.'"

In October 1955, shortly after Parks returned from Tennessee and resumed her work at the Montgomery Fair department store, another young black woman—18-year-old Mary Louise Smith—was arrested on a city bus, but Nixon felt that she was no more suitable as an appellant in a federal appeal than Colvin had been. Smith's father was an alcoholic and the family lived in a rural shack, circumstances Nixon feared would make her case less publicly compelling particularly if members of the family were interviewed by the press. He and the WPC continued their search for the ideal person to test the segregation statutes. Less than three months later, on December 1, 1955, Rosa Parks was arrested. Though she has always maintained that her actions that day were spontaneous, certainly the potential implications of her run-in with the law were not lost on her. "My resistance to being mistreated on the buses and everywhere else was a regular thing with me and not just that day," Parks said, but she has insisted that she did not have herself in mind as the appellant of the proposed test case. "In fact," she said in her autobiography, "if I had let myself think too deeply about what might happen to me, I might have gotten off the bus. But I chose to remain."

"I was thinking," Parks said later, "that the only way to let them know I felt I was being mistreated was to do just what I did—resist the order. I had not thought about it and I had taken no previous resolution until it happened, and then I simply decided that I would not get up. I was tired, but I was usually tired at the end of the day, and I was not feeling well, but then there were many days that I had not felt well. I had felt for a long time, that if I was ever told to get up so a white person could sit, that I would refuse to do so."

Reflecting on that moment of spontaneous defiance and individual courage, the black activist Eldridge Cleaver wrote, "Somewhere in the universe a gear in the machinery shifted." At the Parkses' home, Nixon was exultant. "This is the case," he insisted over and over. "We can boycott the bus lines with

Septima Clark, the director of education at Highlander Folk School, sits with Parks. Clark has said that Parks's time at Highlander gave her the confidence and enthusiasm to claim an active role in the civil rights struggle.

this and at the same time go to the Supreme Court." Concerned for his wife's safety, Ray Parks interjected a note of caution. "Rosa, the white folks will kill you," he warned, but he was ultimately swayed by her determination, as was her mother. "The decision was made by the three of us," Parks told an interviewer in 1989, "my husband, my mother, and me, that I would go on and use my case as a test case challenging segregation on the buses."

RALLYING TO THE CAUSE

Word of Parks's arrest spread quickly throughout Montgomery's black community. From Fred Gray, the city's most successful black attorney, Jo Ann Robinson learned of the arrest late that Thursday night. Though it was near midnight, Robinson did not wait for Parks to approve the boycott. She was in over-drive and spent the night cutting stencils for the boycott announcement at her place of employment. With the help of John Cannon, a fellow employee at the black college, thirty-five thousand flyers were mimeographed calling for Montgomery's black citizens to boycott the city buses on Monday, December 5, the day of Parks's trial. Her only concern was retribution against the school if whites found out.

In the early morning hours before sunrise, in the midst of her work, she called Nixon, who had returned home from the Parks residence to make some calculations. "I went home that night," he remembered later, "and took out a slide rule and a sheet of paper and I put Montgomery in the center of that sheet and I learned that there wasn't a single spot in Montgomery a man couldn't walk to work if he really wanted to. I said it ain't no reason in the world why we should lose the boycott because people couldn't get to work."

The two agreed that Parks was the perfect person to rally the community behind the definitive action that Robinson had been planning for such a long time. "We had planned the protest long before Mrs. Parks was arrested," Robinson later said. "There had been so many things that happened, that the black women had been embarrassed over, and they were ready to explode."

Parks later downplayed her own significance in the events that followed, saying, "If everybody else had been happy and

IN HER OWN WORDS...

Parks wrote in her autobiography *My Story*:

Maybe the habit of protecting my little brother helped me learn to protect myself. I do know that I had a very strong sense of what was fair. That attitude got me into trouble sometimes.

doing well, my arrest wouldn't have made a difference at all." But Robinson felt that her role was critical: "Mrs. Parks had the caliber of character we needed to get the city to rally behind us." Robinson delivered the leaflets after her ten o'clock class to her brigade of elementary school through college students. "Most people got the message, but there were outlying areas that didn't," *Voices of Freedom* quoted Robinson about disseminating the flyers throughout the black sections of the city.

At least one resident of Montgomery began her own personal boycott on Friday morning, December 2. "When I awoke the next morning and realized I had to go to work and it was pouring down rain," Parks said, "the first thing I thought about was the fact that I never would ride a segregated bus again. That was my decision for me and not necessarily for anybody else." Before she took a taxicab to work that morning, Parks called the phone number her cell mate at the jail had given her and asked the woman's brother to go visit her.

While Parks, much to the surprise of her boss, was arriving for work at Montgomery Fair on Friday, Nixon was contacting the Reverend Ralph Abernathy, one of Montgomery's most dynamic young Baptist ministers, about the plans for the boycott. In Montgomery, as elsewhere in the South, the church was the dominant institution within black society, and Nixon recognized that any organized, large-scale protest would have little chance of succeeding without the support of the city's black clergymen. The ministers, Nixon said, "had their hands on the black masses." (For additional information on Ralph Abernathy, enter "Ralph Abernathy" into any search engine and browse the sites listed.)

Similar reasoning caused Nixon to bypass the NAACP in organizing the boycott. For the boycott to work, it had to be a grassroots, mass movement that could draw on the support of every segment of the Montgomery black community. The NAACP was a highly structured, centralized organization that drew most of its support from the more educated and affluent members of the black community and offered little opportunity for group participation. When Nixon did contact the local NAACP chapter about the protest, "the man who was the president of the NAACP at the time said, 'Bro Nixon, I'll have to talk to New York [the organization's national headquarters] about that.' I said, man, we ain't got time for that."

E.D. Nixon, who had to work Friday night (he was a Pullman railroad porter), enlisted Abernthy's assistance bringing together the city's most important black ministers, including H.H. Hubbard, W.J. Powell, L. Roy Bennett, Edgar French, and the new pastor of the Dexter Avenue Baptist Church, Martin Luther King, Jr. to participate in planning unified action. King asked for time to think about the situation before committing and according to one account received a little persuasion to support the activity from Abernathy. They met that evening at King's Dexter church without Nixon. Over the course of the next several days, these individuals and several others formed a new organization to coordinate the boycott, the Montgomery Improvement Association (MIA). After some debate, a consensus was reached that the articulate and well-educated King should be the MIA president.

On Friday night, December 2, the group decided to issue a revised version of Robinson's manifesto. It reiterated the plans for the boycott and announced a mass meeting of the Montgomery black community, to be held at the Holt Street Baptist Church on Monday night, December 5, for the purpose of determining whether the boycott should be extended beyond that day. While the Reverend W.J. Powell contacted the city's 10 black taxicab companies to persuade them to reduce their fare to 10 cents (the same as the bus fare) on Monday, King and Abernathy spent Saturday night prowling Montgomery's nightclubs and saloons. Their purpose was to inform those who were unlikely to be found in church on Sunday morning about the boycott; as Abernathy put it, the MIA needed the "sinners" as well as the "saints."

Their reception in the city's many joints—most of them, in Abernathy's words, "small, wooden-frame buildings, no more than lopsided shacks jammed with tables and chairs"—was enthusiastic. "By the time we had visited all the night spots we knew," Abernathy wrote in his autobiography, "we were reasonably certain the 'sinners' would be with us." On Sunday morning, those "saints" who had not yet gotten the word heard it spoken to them by their ministers from the pulpit.

The MIA's work in relaying information about the boycott was further aided by a sympathetic white newspaper editor for the Montgomery *Advertiser*, Joe Azbell, to whom Nixon leaked "the hottest story he'd ever written." The boycott story, which

Jo Ann Robinson's Flyer Calling For a Bus Boycott:

This is for Monday, December 5, 1955

Another Negro woman has been arrested and thrown into jail because she refused to get up out of her seat on the bus for a white person to sit down.

It is the second time since the Claudette Colbert [Colvin] case that a Negro woman has been arrested for the same thing. This has to be stopped.

Negroes have rights, too, for if Negroes did not ride the buses, they could not operate. Three-fourths of the riders are Negroes, yet we are arrested, or have to stand over empty seats. If we do not do something to stop these arrests, they will continue. The next time it may be you, or your daughter, or mother.

This woman's case will come up on Monday. We are, therefore, asking every Negro to stay off the buses Monday in protest of the arrest and trial. Don't ride the buses to work, to town, to school, or anywhere on Monday.

You can afford to stay out of school for one day if you have no other way to go except by bus.

You can also afford to stay out of town for one day. If you work, take a cab, or walk. But please, children and grown-ups don't ride the bus at all on Monday. Please stay off of all buses Monday.

quoted liberally from the new leaflet and also mentioned the Monday night mass meeting, appeared on the front page of the Sunday edition of the newspaper. By Sunday night, the MIA was quite certain that virtually every member of the black community had been informed about the boycott.

Surprised by all the activity in the community following her arrest, Parks continued with her plans for that weekend. She had spent a lot of time arranging to have a guest speaker from Birmingham address her NAACP youth group on Saturday morning, but her disappointment that so few children showed up for the workshop faded when she discovered that many of her missing students were among the 200 volunteers who spent the day distributing handbills about the boycott. "That's why I love young people so," she later remarked. "There's a time for meetings and a time for speeches—a very important time—but there is also a time for action, and not the speeches. It is to youth that all of us must look. There is still a great deal for all of us to do, and those who will not dare themselves should certainly support the young people who will."

THE BOYCOTT BEGINS

At 5:30 A.M. on Monday, December 5, the driver of the first bus to pull into the Court Square stop was met by a big, white cardboard sign tacked to the wall of the bus shed. Printed with shoe polish, the sign read, "People, don't ride the bus today. Don't ride it, for freedom." Blacks gathered at the stop to wait silently for cab rides, while others walked quietly to work; traffic was heavy as black cabs drove by filled with passengers. Across town, Martin Luther King, Jr., and his wife, Coretta, rose at dawn to see how many people were on the 6:00 A.M. bus that stopped in front of their home on South Jackson Street. "Martin, come quickly!" Coretta called from the window to her husband, who was in the kitchen, pouring coffee. "It's empty!" Normally one of the most crowded in the city, the South Jackson Street bus was empty. Instead, the sidewalks were crowded with pedestrians, cars passed by overloaded with people, students hitched rides, and one man even rode by on a mule. The next two buses drove by, and they were also empty "as naked as can be" in the words of one black Montgomery resident. An hour later, King and Abernathy watched a similar scene from Abernathy's home.

For several hours, King and Abernathy drove around Montgomery's streets, enjoying the glorious sight of empty city buses vainly making their rounds. Their own unscientific methods yielded a count of just 10 black passengers on the city buses. But no matter what method of figuring was used, it was clear that compliance with the boycott was almost total.

6

"I Was Not Alone"

For Rosa Parks the sight of the empty buses rolling by her house that Monday morning would become the most vivid memory of her life. At precisely 9:00 A.M. dressed in a straight, long-sleeved black dress with a white collar and cuffs, white gloves, and a small black velvet hat with pearls on it, and carrying a black purse, she presented herself, with her attorney, Fred Gray, before Judge John B. Scott of the city court of Montgomery, Alabama. Within five minutes, she had been convicted of violating Alabama state law regarding segregation on buses and fined $10 (plus $4 for court costs).

To the delighted surprise of Nixon, Abernathy, and others who accompanied Parks, the courthouse steps and hallways were filled with black supporters 500 at least, maybe more, an unprecedented sight in segregated Montgomery. "The one thing I appreciated," Parks later remembered in 1989, "was the fact that when so many others, by the hundreds and by the thousands, joined in, there was a kind of lifting of a burden from me individually. I could feel that whatever my individual desires were to be free, I was not alone. There were many others who felt the same way." As she entered the courthouse, Parks could hear the high-pitched voice of one of the girls from her NAACP youth group. "Oh, she's so sweet," the girl cried over and over. "They've messed with the wrong one now. They've messed with the wrong one now."

THE STRENGTH OF AN ARMY—THE WILL OF GOD

For Nixon, the gathering at the courthouse represented his first real inkling that Parks's arrest had unleashed forces beyond even the most hopeful expectations that he shared with Robinson and other like-minded individuals. For others a similar realization would be triggered by the scene that night at the Holt Street Baptist Church. The church had been chosen as the site of the meeting because of its size—1,000 worshipers could fit inside—and every seat was filled by five o'clock, two hours before the scheduled start of the mass meeting.

Traveling together, Abernathy and King, who just that afternoon had been chosen president of the MIA, became caught up in traffic while still five blocks away from the church. Cars were parked in every available space and at crazy angles across sidewalks and on lawns. The ministers abandoned their vehicle and began to make their way on foot through the ever-growing throng of silent, solemn blacks who surrounded the filled church for several blocks in every direction. As they reached the building itself, they noticed that loudspeakers had been strung up outside to broadcast the proceedings to the orderly crowd. King realized as he shouldered his way through the crowd outside that there was no chance the boycott would be confined to a single day. "By now my doubts concerning the success of our venture were dispelled," King recalled in his book *Stride Toward Freedom: The Montgomery Story*. "The question of calling off the protest was now academic. The enthusiasm of these thousands of people swept everything along like an onrushing tidal wave."

Abernathy's memories, as related in *And the Walls Came Tumbling Down*, were more detailed:

"As we drove through the darkened streets we told each other the people would turn out, but we didn't really believe it. About five blocks away from the church we saw cars parked on both sides of the street; and when we were about three blocks away, the driveways and front yards were also filled up. First we thought it was a party, then Martin and I came to the same conclusion simultaneously—somebody extremely important had died, the head deacon or the preacher himself.

"I turned at the next corner and drove away from the church until I finally found a space and parked. When we got out we heard the first sound—a low growl somewhere in the distance. It took a moment before we realized that what we heard was a huge crowd of people, not shouting or cheering the way they do in a football stadium, but talking among themselves. I think at that moment, I realized what it was, and I felt my spine tingle.

"When we rounded the last corner we saw them, milling in the dark shadows of the overhanging oaks—hordes of people, a whole army of them, more people than I had ever seen in my life. As my eyes scanned the horizon in both directions all I saw was the crowd. It seemed to spill into the next neighborhood on all sides. . . .

"I heard Martin mutter something under his breath, an expression of surprise. As we approached someone saw us and called out, then they all turned toward us and began to make a pathway for us to pass through.

"Then the crowd started applauding, politely at first, then louder and louder. Finally they were applauding wildly and cheering. . . . When we entered the church the noise was magnified ten times. They were crying out of a sense of newfound freedom, not cheering us so much as cheering themselves for what they had done that day, what we all had done. I don't think I have ever heard a more joyous sound in my life."

From her seat with several ministers and scheduled speakers on a platform behind the pulpit, Parks joined with the audience in several prayers and hymns before listening to Nixon's fiery exhortation: "You who are afraid, you better get your hat and coat and go home," he warned the crowd. "This is going to be a long drawn-out affair. I want to tell you something: For years and years I've been talking about how I didn't want the children who came along behind me to suffer the indignities that I've suffered all these years. Well, I've changed my mind— I want to enjoy some of that freedom myself."

Editor Joe Azbell said when he entered the church, "I was the first white person there. The preachers were preaching as I came in, and that audience was so on fire that at last this was going to be lifted off them. And I recognized that. There was a spirit there that no one could ever capture again in a movie or anything else, because it was so powerful. The next day, in a special column, I wrote that this was the beginning of a flame that would go across America."

A NEW LEADER EMERGES

That afternoon, at the meeting of the MIA at which the organization had adopted its name and King had been chosen as its president, Nixon had been equally blunt when some ministers seemed frightened by the prospect of addressing the crowd that night, for fear that their names and pictures would appear in the newspaper, making them subject to white retaliation. "I am just ashamed of you," Nixon had said then. "You said that God has called you to lead the people and now you are afraid and gone to pieces because the man tells you that the newspapermen will be here and your pictures might come out in the newspaper. Somebody has got to be hurt in this thing and if you preachers are not the leaders, then we have to pray that God will send us some more leaders."

Soon, it was King's turn. Like most of those in the crowd, Parks did not know very much about the new leader of the MIA, although she had heard him speak several months earlier at an NAACP meeting. Aware, now more than ever, of the magnitude of the occasion, King was somewhat nervous about his speech. Busy with other boycott matters throughout the day, he had had no more than 20 unoccupied minutes in which to compose some remarks, and during that brief interlude he had become "possessed by fear" and "obsessed by a feeling of inadequacy." Usually, King wrote out his sermons in their entirety before delivering them, but he approached the pulpit this night with no more than a few scrawled notes on a single piece of paper.

"We are here this evening," King began, his mellifluous, deep voice slow paced, "for serious business. We are here in a general sense because first and foremost we are American citizens. . . . But we are here in a specific sense because of the bus situation in Montgomery. We are here because we are determined to get the situation corrected."

The specific situation, King reminded his listeners, was not new. "The problem has existed over endless years. . . . On so many occasions, Negroes have been intimidated and humiliated and oppressed because of the sheer fact that they were Negroes." There was no need for his listeners to hear him recite the history of such abuses, King then said, his voice rising and his speech becoming more rapid, although he paused briefly after each clause for emphasis, "but at least one stands before us now with glaring dimensions. Just the other day, just last Thursday to be exact, one of the finest citizens in Montgomery—not one of the finest Negro citizens but one of the finest citizens in Montgomery—was taken from a bus and carried to jail and arrested because she refused to get up to give her seat to a white person. . . . Mrs. Rosa Parks is a fine person. And since it had to happen, I'm happy it happened to a person like Mrs. Parks, for nobody can doubt the boundless outreach of her integrity. Nobody can doubt the height of her character, nobody can doubt the depth of her Christian commitment and devotion to the teachings of Jesus. . . . And just because she refused to get up, she was arrested." The crowd, both inside and outside the church, now punctuated each declaration with "yes" and "amen" and "that's right."

"And, you know, my friends," King continued, "there comes a time when people get tired of being trampled over by the iron feet of oppression." As Parks's arrest had triggered the long-suppressed outrage of the black citizens of the South, so King's inspired oratory had touched a nerve; the tumultuous, spontaneous applause and stamping of feet that followed this declaration overwhelmed the speaker into a temporary silence and, according to Taylor Branch, author of *Parting the Waters: America in the King Years,* "rolled on and on, like a wave that refused to break . . . the giant cloud of noise shook the building and refused to go away."

"There comes a time, my friends," King continued, "when people get tired of being flung across the abyss of humiliation where they experience the bleakness of nagging despair. There comes a time when people get tired of being pushed out of the glittering sunlight of life's July and left standing amidst the piercing chill of an Alpine November. We are here, we are here this evening because we're tired now."

Again, the tumult from the crowd halted him. Though the time for patience had passed, King told his now rapt listeners, their protest must be a nonviolent one; the hatred and violence that had been used by their oppressors to keep them subjugated must not be utilized now by themselves in the service of freedom: "Now let us say that we are not here advocating violence. We have overcome that. . . . The only weapon that we have here in our hands this evening is the weapon of protest. . . . My friends, don't let anybody make us feel that we ought to be compared in our actions with the Ku Klux Klan. . . . There will be no crosses burned at any bus stops in Montgomery. There will be no white persons pulled out of their homes and taken out to some distant road and murdered. There will be nobody among us who will stand up and defy the Constitution of this nation."

But King also emphasized that nonviolence should not be misinterpreted as a lack of commitment to the rightness of their cause: "My friends, I want it to be known that we're going to work with grim and firm determination to gain justice on the buses in this city. And we are not wrong, we are not wrong in what we are doing. If we are wrong, then the Supreme Court of this nation is wrong. If we are wrong, the Constitution of the United States is wrong. If we are wrong, God Almighty is wrong. If we are wrong, Jesus of Nazareth was merely a utopian dreamer and never came down to earth. If we are wrong, justice is a lie. And we are determined here in Montgomery to work and fight until justice runs down like water and righteousness like a mighty stream. . . . We are going to work together. Right here in Montgomery, when the history books are written in the future, somebody will have to say, 'There lived a race of people, black people, fleecy locks and black complexion, of people who had the moral courage to stand up for their rights.'"

It took 15 minutes after King's speech for the audience to calm down enough to let the meeting begin. Parks was then introduced to the crowd and received a standing ovation, but she had determined in advance not to speak; "you have had enough and you have said enough and you don't have to speak," Nixon had told her. Abernathy then informed the crowd about the demands that the MIA intended to present to the city and the bus company, which did not even amount to a challenge to segregated seating; the MIA asked only for courteous treatment of black passengers, the hiring of black bus drivers, and the adoption of the segregated system of seating used in other southern cities, whereby blacks filled the available seating in an empty bus from the rear and whites from the front until all the seats had been taken.

Rosa Parks's decision to stay in her seat on a segregated Alabama bus sparked the Montgomery bus boycotts and many other protests to follow. Parks is seen here arriving on February 24, 1956, at court to be arraigned in the bus boycott. She was one of over one hundred boycott participants indicted for breaking an Alabama statute that prohibited boycotting.

A question was posed: Should the boycott end? "No! No!" people shouted. "This is just the beginning!" someone yelled, to thunderous applause. When Abernathy asked the audience to "stand if you want to continue the boycott and make the demands," the entire congregation rose, and the crowd outside screamed, "Yes!" As the crowd dispersed, its individual members each took with them a tremendous feeling of joyousness and pride, a spirit perhaps best typified by Mother Pollard, an old woman who had participated in the boycott that day. As she walked slowly to work that December morning, her minister came by in his car and offered her a ride. Was she getting tired? he solicitously asked. "My soul has been tired for a long time," Mother Pollard replied. "Now my feet are tired and my soul is resting."

7

"Montgomery Is On Trial"

Following her arrest Rosa Parks was scorned by many of her co-workers at the Montgomery Fair department store. Some of the women who worked in the same room with her would no longer speak to her, while others she passed while walking through the store would put their heads down or look the other way to avoid acknowledging her. Parks's job at the store lasted only five weeks after her arrest; in January 1956 she was told that the store would be closing its tailoring shop and that her job had been terminated. Ray Parks lost his job at the barbershop at Maxwell Field when the white proprietor of the shop issued an order that there was to be no discussion of the bus boycott or of Rosa Parks in his establishment. Ray Parks quit, saying that he refused to work anywhere that his wife's name could not be mentioned, and Rosa took in sewing at home to earn money. She volunteered the majority of her newfound free time as a member of the MIA executive board, working with the organizers of the bus boycott.

The boycott meant considerable hardship for most of the black residents of Montgomery. Some had to rise as early as 3:00 A.M. to walk as far as six miles to work in the morning.

During the first days of the boycott, black cabs offered cheap fares until city officials began enforcing an ordinance that mandated certain minimum rates for taxis. Then, blacks who owned their own cars started carrying people to and from work for a small gasoline fee of 15 cents per person, until the police began stopping drivers for operating an unlicensed taxi service.

ORGANIZING FOR THE DURATION

In response, the MIA transportation committee organized a volunteer car pool of drivers and automobiles. Various black businesses in Montgomery's downtown area and black residences were designated as pickup and dispatch stations. The committee produced thousands of leaflets, including a timetable and a map of Montgomery showing the location of 48 dispatch and 42 pickup stations. The black Citizens Club of Montgomery, where the transportation committee oversaw its daily operation, became the hub of the car pool. Clerks at the club answered telephones, directed automobiles to those who could not reach the pickup stations, and kept the cars running smoothly. MIA bookkeepers and secretaries worked together at long tables inside the club, handling correspondence, bills for gasoline and car repairs, and payments to the drivers for the use of their cars.

Car-pool rides were free for virtually everyone participating in the boycott; a small fee was charged only for those destinations at the outermost limits of the city. Three hundred and twenty-five car owners volunteered the use of their automobiles in the car pool, and many people volunteered to be drivers, usually from five until eight in the morning or from five until

Rosa Parks with E.D. Nixon, former president of the Alabama
NAACP, at the Montgomery courthouse for the bus boycott
trial on March 19, 1956. Over 30,000 blacks participated in
the boycott which lasted 381 days.

nine in the evening, the peak hours for people traveling to and
from work. Parks worked as a dispatcher for the car pool, taking
calls from people who needed rides and helping coordinate
a homemade transportation system so effective that even the
city police commissioner, Clyde Sellers, admitted that it worked
with "military precision."

franchise, Mayor W.A. Gayle was also urging white residents of the city not to support the boycott. City commissioner Frank Parks proclaimed, "Negroes will not be allowed to destroy the public transportation system of the city of Montgomery" and reported enthusiastically that many local businessmen had promised to lay off black employees "who were being used as NAACP instruments in this boycott."

TAKING THE HITS

Meanwhile, Police Commissioner Sellers orchestrated a policy of harassment: Police routinely stopped the church station wagons and car-pool vehicles, checking for proper driver's licenses, insurance, and registration, and issuing tickets for even the most minor bureaucratic and traffic infractions, such as carrying a "mutilated" license or "staying too long" or "too short" at a stop sign. Drivers were arrested for carrying too many people in the front seat of their cars. Police handed out violations for misaligned headlights or poor brakes, forcing the passengers to abandon the vehicle and pay for a city wrecker to tow it away for repairs. Jo Ann Robinson, for example, a notoriously careful driver, was issued 17 summonses in the span of a few weeks. To make matters worse, Montgomery insurance companies began to refuse to insure MIA vehicles. The largest black owned insurance company, Atlanta Life in King's old Sweet Auburn neighborhood of Atlanta, Georgia, formed a consortium of insurers to solve that problem. (During the course of the boycott, all three city commissioners—Gayle, Parks, and Sellers—joined the White Citizens Council, a civic group with supremacy objectives, similar to the Klan, dedicated to the preservation of segregation in Alabama "before it is too late.")

On January 23, the City Commission announced an end to negotiations with the MIA until blacks were ready to stop the boycott. "White people do not care whether Negroes ever ride the buses again," Mayor Gayle said. "We are not going to be a part of any program that will get Negroes to ride buses again at the destruction of our heritage and way of life." Three days later, as he transported boycotters in an MIA station wagon, Martin Luther King, Jr., who had been plagued nightly by phone calls threatening his life and that of his wife and newborn daughter, was arrested for speeding, although he was soon released on his own recognizance after hundreds of black supporters surrounded the city jail.

Admittedly frightened by the arrest and jailing—"when I was first arrested in Montgomery, I thought I was going to be lynched"—and the death threats, and discouraged by the long road ahead of him and the boycotters, King "was ready to give up," he said later. Thus far in his young life, he had enjoyed what he regarded as a generally privileged existence. "I didn't have to worry about anything," he remembered in *Stride Toward Freedom.* "I have a marvelous mother and father. They went out of their way to provide everything for their children. . . . I went right on through school; I never had to drop out to work or anything. And you know, I was about to conclude that life had been wrapped up for me in a Christmas package." Like Parks, King had not aspired to leadership in the civil rights movement, and he had no more wished than she or anyone else to suffer unnecessarily; circumstances, and the dictates of their conscience, had forced them to take the actions they had.

"Everything was done [for me]," he recalled of his life before Montgomery. "Things were solved. But one day after finishing school, I was called to a little church, down in Montgomery, Alabama. And I started preaching there. Things were going well in that church, it was a marvelous experience. But one day a year later, a lady by the name of Rosa Parks decided that she wasn't going to take it any longer. . . . It was the beginning of a movement."

Having just received another death threat "If you aren't out of this town in three days, we're going to blow your brains out, and blow up your house"—King sat up alone in his home, thinking. "With my cup of coffee sitting untouched before me, I tried to think of a way to move out of the picture without appearing a coward," he recalled later. Despairing, torn between fear and responsibility, he began to pray. "And it seemed at that moment I could hear an inner voice saying to me, 'Martin Luther, stand up for righteousness. Stand up for justice. Stand up for truth. And, lo, I will be with you, even until the end of the world. . . .' Almost at once my fears began to go. My uncertainty disappeared."

Another voice provided further reassurance. On the night of January 30, King spoke at a mass meeting at the First Baptist Church, where Ralph Abernathy was the minister. King's speech, he admitted later, was not one of his best, and when he concluded, Mother Pollard, now enshrined as one of the boycott's many elderly "walking heroes," slowly approached the podium and addressed him. "Come here, son," she said, reaching out to embrace him. "Something is wrong with you. You didn't talk strong tonight." King tried to reassure her. "Now you can't fool me," she responded, then spoke again as he began another response. "I done told you we is with you all the way. But even if we ain't with you, God's gonna take care of you." King began to weep, and once again he felt his fears lifted. A few minutes later, he learned from Abernathy that his house had been bombed.

Within minutes, a crowd of more than 300 people, most of them angry blacks, had assembled outside the King home. The bomb had landed on the porch of the house and shattered a front window, split a section of the porch, and left a hole in the porch floor. King's wife, Coretta, their two-month-old daughter, Yoki and a visitor, Mary Lucy Williams, managed to escape injury. With Sellers and Gayle on the scene, condemning the bombing and proclaiming their determination to catch the assailant, the crowd grew agitated, until King emerged from the wreckage to urge restraint. There must be no retaliation, he emphasized: "We are not advocating violence. We want to love our enemies. Be good to them. Love them and let them know you love them." Then he pointed out that the movement that had begun with the brave act of a single, perhaps otherwise unremarkable woman, and had been carried forward by the eloquence and courage of a young, initially reluctant minister, was now much bigger than any of the individuals involved: "I want it to be known the length and breadth of this land that if I am stopped, this movement will not stop. If I am stopped, our work will not stop. For what we are doing is right. What we are doing is just. And God is with us."

PUTTING SEGREGATION TO THE SUPREME TEST

"It was bigger than bus seats now," King was later quoted as telling his father, when he arrived in Montgomery early in the morning following the bombing, determined to bring his son and his family home to Atlanta to safety. Later that morning, February 1, 1956, Fred Gray, with the approval of the MIA and the advice of Durr and several NAACP lawyers, filed suit in federal court, seeking to overturn segregation on public transportation in Montgomery as unconstitutional and incompatible with the Supreme Court's ruling in *Brown* v. *Board of Education*. Parks's "test case," for various reasons, had become less than ideal: The various appeals necessary to move it to the Supreme Court, Gray and the MIA leadership had become aware, could take years, especially if the state chose to use delaying tactics. It was also possible that the court might decide the case on the fact that there was no other seat available to Parks, rather than rendering a decision on the constitutional validity of segregation. The federal suit represented an escalation of the boycott, for initially the boycotters had sought only more courteous treatment and a more equitable form of segregation; now, through the federal lawsuit, they were seeking to abolish segregation altogether. This was a class suit, pulling together several of Parks's carefully documented bus incidences. As *Browder* v. *Gayle* moved forward, Colvin and others would have their day in court—the highest court in the land.

For whites like Virginia Durr the boycott brought a kind of relief, "The boycott took off some of the terrible load of guilt that white southerners have lived under for so many generations, such a terrible load of shame and guilt that we won't acknowledge," and then she conveyed another type of black-white ploy. A "terrible schizophrenia," she called it in *Voices of Freedom.* "At least under the Nazis they never even pretended to like the Jews, but in the South it was always that terrible hypocrisy. You know, 'We love the blacks and understand them and they love us.' Both sides were playing roles, which were pure hypocrisy. So I thought the boycott was absolutely marvelous."

For a different side of white Alabama, wrote Branch, the "suit was the social equivalent of atomic warfare." That night, a bomb exploded on Nixon's lawn.

Several days later, Gray's draft status was changed from exempt to active; after his induction, there would be just one black attorney left in Montgomery. The city deputized out-of-work bus drivers and sent them to patrol the car-pool pickup and dispatch stations, where they harassed black drivers; policemen, or men dressed as policemen, destroyed black automobiles, sprayed yards with chemicals to destroy flowers, splattered paint on homes, tossed nails onto driveways and roads, and even threw human excrement on porches. White teenagers drove through black neighborhoods and tossed balloons filled with urine at pedestrians; one carload of teenage boys tried to catch a black boy's head in a noose they flung from their car. Whites in speeding cars also threw rotten eggs and vegetables at blacks as they walked to work. One black boy was seriously injured by a brick thrown from a passing car; another was jumped on and beaten unconscious while walking home from a mass meeting. Confederate flags appeared everywhere, as if to signal that the ways of the old South were still alive.

Rosa Parks was among the many individuals specifically targeted for harassment. Day and night, callers phoned her home to threaten her. "You're the cause of all this. You should

Browder v. Gayle

Attorneys Fred Gray and Charles Langford filed a class action suit in U.S. district court on behalf of primary plaintiffs, Aurelia S. Browder, Susie McDonald, Claudette Colvin, Mary Louis Smith, Jeanetta Reese, and Rosa Parks, alleging that segregated busing laws in Montgomery, Alabama, violated the Constitution and laws of the United States. According to Parks only three plaintiffs stayed in the case until the end—seemingly Browder, Colvin, and herself.

People of color in the United States had found friends to justice and Constitutional freedom in some federal courts. The Middle District of Alabama Northern Division turned out to be one of them when Judges Rives and Johnson ruled that the segregation codes for the state of Alabama and city of Montgomery public transportation denied and deprived Negro citizens of equal protection and due process granted them under the Fourteenth Amendment. Judge Lynne dissented except to concur with allowing continued enforcement of segregation until the appeal was underway.

The decision was appealed to the U.S. Supreme Court, which upheld its lower court ruling on November 13, 1956. On December 21 of the same year that decision was signed into law, the 381-day Montgomery Boycott ended. *Brown* v. *Board of Education*, decided two years earlier, served as the wrecking crane against Jim Crow in schools, and then *Browder* v. *Gayle* became the wrecking ball laying waste to similar laws for public accommodations.

It takes considerable time for the U.S. Supreme Court to overturn a previous ruling and after decades of NAACP cases, it finally did just that. Changing laws, however, cannot change the hearts or minds of people filled with hate and determined to maintain their preferential status in America. Before the final *Browder* ruling, the Alabama legislature voted to request federal dollars to relocate African Americans out of the South, 101 members of Congress signed the "Southern Manifesto" against desegregation, and the Georgia General Assembly tried to impeach selected U.S. Supreme Court judges on June 19, 1956, but the legislators were unsuccessful. Afterward when desegregated buses and their black passengers in Montgomery became targets for drive by shootings and harassment, the black community once again stood strong and could not be coerced out of integration.

be killed" was a typical message. One woman called to inquire whether Parks had lost her job; when Parks said yes the woman said she was very sorry, then laughed until Parks finally hung up the phone. Seeking to spare her increasing stomach ulcers, Ray Parks and Parks's mother answered most of the calls, but the threats made Parks's husband so nervous that he eventually suffered a nervous breakdown. Parks was not as easily frightened. "Well, you have to die sometime," she said. "If this boycott happened to be attributed to me and my activity, and they killed me, then I would just be dead."

LEGAL BACKLASH

On Tuesday, February 21, a specially impaneled grand jury indicted 115 of the boycott's so-called leaders under a 1921 Alabama State statute that prohibited boycotts. It was the largest mass indictment in the history of Montgomery County; among those indicted—only 89 were ever actually arrested, 24 of them ministers—were King, Abernathy, Nixon, and Rosa Parks. The grand jurors' report stated that "distrust, dislike, and hatred are being taught in a community which for more than a generation has enjoyed exemplary race relations." The way to continue such "exemplary race relations" was simple, the report implied: "We intend to maintain separate facilities in schools, public transportation, and elsewhere."

The charges only strengthened the solidarity of the black community. Following Nixon's lead, on Wednesday, February 22, many of those indicted (as well as numerous supporters) walked to the courthouse to present themselves for arrest rather than wait for the police to apprehend them. With so many of the boycotters present, the scene at the courthouse soon resembled, in the words of one reporter, "old home week." At a mass meeting the next night, the community approved Abernathy's suggestion to make Friday, February 24, the day of arraignment for those indicted, a "carless" day. As a gesture of solidarity with those arrested, all of black

Montgomery would conduct its business on foot; hearses, doctors' cars, and ambulances were to be the only motorized vehicles used on Prayer Pilgrimage Day, as Abernathy designated it. The indictments and arrests, editor Grover Hall, Jr., opined in the pages of the Montgomery *Advertiser*, were "the dumbest act that had ever been done in Montgomery"; in addition to further solidifying black support for the boycott, the arrests brought the protesters and their leaders, especially King, an unprecedented amount of national media attention and thousands of dollars in outside donations.

As it turned out, King was the only one of the indicted boycott leaders to ever go to trial. On Thursday, March 22, after four days of proceedings, he was pronounced guilty and was sentenced to either a $500 fine (plus $500 in court costs) or 386 days of hard labor. The conviction made King a martyr ("Here is the man who today was nailed to the cross for you and me" was how he was introduced to the audience at the mass meeting held at Holt Street Baptist Church the night of his conviction), became front-page news in such important periodicals as the *New York Times*, added to King's growing fame, and made Montgomery the subject of much ridicule in places that prided themselves on being more enlightened. The backlash caused legal proceedings on the other cases, including Parks's, to be dropped. "The Negroes are not on trial here," one minister said of the indictments. "Montgomery is on trial."

NO TURNING AROUND

Despite the mayor's order to fire all black maids who participated in the boycott, white women did not want to lose their help and some actually transported their workers. When questioned by husbands or authorities the lies told became the composition of imaginative black and white interplay. As Virginia Durr quoted one woman's thought about innocuous tales of how she got to work, "Well, you know, when you have your hand in the lion's mouth, the best thing to do is pat it on the head."

With the white political leadership of Montgomery adamantly refusing any hint of compromise or settlement—even after a U.S. Supreme Court ruling outlawed segregated seating on buses in Columbia, South Carolina, the Montgomery commissioners announced that their city would continue to enforce segregation—the boycott continued; its focus was now May 11, when the federal suit would be heard by a three-judge panel. The MIA was just "waiting and hoping," King said. "Our whole strategy is based on the May 11 trial."

Meanwhile, Parks, who had attained some measure of fame as a result of the publicity accorded the boycott, began to travel around the country, often in the company of Nixon and A. Philip Randolph, giving fund-raising speeches at various NAACP branches, schools, unions, and churches. Her appearances were usually quite effective; Rosa Parks symbolized the entire civil rights movement going on in Montgomery, Alabama. The money she raised was used primarily to purchase station wagons for the boycott. When she was in Montgomery, Parks would dispense the clothing and shoes that had been sent to the MIA from supporters around the country to aid the many boycotters who had lost their jobs. She and her husband also organized a cleanup squad to help repair the damage done to people's homes by bombs. One black section of Montgomery became known as Dynamite Hill because of all the bombs that had been thrown at the houses there.

On June 4, 1956, by a two-to-one vote, the three-judge federal panel ruled that Montgomery's segregated seating ordinances were unconstitutional under the Fourteenth Amendment and the Supreme Court's ruling in *Brown* v. *Board of Education*. Five more months of demonstrations and protest followed this initial legal victory, until, on November 13, the U.S. Supreme Court, acting on Montgomery's appeal, affirmed the ruling of the three-judge panel. Although white Montgomery continued to resist—the Supreme Court's rejection of the city's final appeal was followed by a bombing campaign in which several black churches and the homes of ministers were destroyed, a shotgun blast ripped through the door of King's home one night while his family slept, and snipers fired regularly at the newly integrated buses—the boycotters had won.

JUST DECISION

The Supreme Court's order implementing desegregated seating was served on Montgomery city officials on Thursday, December 20, 1956. The following morning, integrated bus service began in Montgomery with a fare increase of five cents. Nixon, Abernathy, Gray, and a white minister named Glenn Smiley were present when the first city bus rolled up at the Jackson Avenue stop outside King's home at 5:45 A.M. There, King and the others boarded, with King conspicuously taking a seat next to Smiley near the front of the bus.

Parks's mother was not feeling well. So she decided to stay home to care for her, but the press was hungry for pictures of her. They persisted until later that morning she agreed to be driven downtown where she boarded a couple of empty buses, including one driven by Blake. Inside each, *Look* magazine photographers snapped pictures with a white newsman seated behind her. She said that she could have done without the exposure. Unlike many of Montgomery's blacks, Parks was somewhat less than jubilant now that the boycott was over. Victory had been achieved at a high cost—bombings, property damage, lost jobs—that indicated the intensity of white resistance to significant change in the South, and Parks, like King and other leaders, had been made aware that the struggle over integrated public transportation was just the beginning. King, for example, was now declaring the movement's dedication to achieving equality at the ballot box—"the chief weapon in our fight for civil rights is the vote"—and to the actual integration of public schools—"that is when our race will gain full equality." "It didn't feel like a victory, actually," Parks said about the end of the boycott. "There still was a great deal to do."

Martin Luther King, Jr., rose to prominence as a civil rights leader through his work leading the Montgomery bus boycott. Here, King stands outside the Montgomery courthouse with other indicted African Americans after being found guilty of conspiring to boycott.

Yet, the change that Parks had inspired was significant and profound. "On December 5 last year [the date of her arrest]," a black citizen of Montgomery said, "the Negro in Montgomery grew from a boy to a man. He'll never be the same again. A white man had always said before, 'Boy, go do this, Boy, do that,' and the Negro jumped and did it. Now he says, 'I don't believe I will,' or he does it, but up straight, looking at the white man. Not a boy anymore. He grew up." A black mother added: "We know now that we're free citizens of the United States. Now we are aiming to become free citizens of Alabama. Our state motto, you know, is, 'We dare defend our rights.' It says nothing about just white rights."

8

Carrying on the Fight

The personal consequences of Rosa Parks's act of individual
courage continued to manifest themselves. Labeled as trouble-
makers, it was impossible for her and her husband to find jobs
in the state. Menacing phone calls were unending, and after
Rosa was threatened by a white man on the street, Ray Parks
began sleeping with his gun nearby. Certain that they would
never again be able to find work in Montgomery, and eager to
escape the city's poisonous racial climate and the hurt from
friends who grew jealous of her international notoriety, she and
her husband accepted her brother Sylvester's offer to help them
relocate to Detroit, Michigan. With its many relatively high-
paying jobs at automobile plants and in related industries,
and freedom from legal segregation, Detroit had attracted
thousands of southern blacks in the years following World
War II. Sylvester McCauley, who worked for the Ford Motor
Company, had not returned to Alabama since the 1940s.

KEEPING HEARTH AND SOUL TOGETHER

Rosa's cousin Thomas Williamson wired $300 for their passage and with $800 raised for them by friends and well-wishers, Ray, Rosa, and her mother left Montgomery for Detroit in the spring of 1957. They settled in an apartment on Euclid Avenue found for them by Sylvester.

Relocation did not immediately make things easier for the Parkses. For one thing finding adequately paying jobs was a challenge. Rosa continued to travel and make appearances for civil rights causes. During one appearance, in Boston, Massachusetts, she met the president of Hampton Institute, an all-black college in Virginia. He offered her a job as hostess of the college's guest and residence house. Rosa took the position, intending that her husband and mother would eventually join her in Virginia. She found a peace in Hampton that she had never known. Working with the young avid minds of the students who adored her was a delight. And for the first time she had responsibility for supervising a staff. If not for the absence of her family those would have been perfect days. She tried to find barbering work for Ray and a suitable family residence but none was available. Overcome by loneliness and plagued by health problems, she returned to Detroit in December 1958 to care for her ailing family and herself.

Though life was in some ways better in the North—Ray Parks had obtained a job an instructor and maintenance man at a barber college and he registered to vote for the first time without being harassed—the Parks family still knew much hardship. Ray's income was inadequate to meet the family's expenditures, and for a time, until Rosa found work as a seamstress at home and later in a clothing factory, the family had to make do with donated clothing and funds.

Despite her own needs, Rosa Parks took time to attend to others. Disappointed, after joining the local NAACP branch, by the lack of solidarity she found among Detroit's blacks, Parks organized her own charity to combat the problems of poverty and homelessness she found in her West Side neighborhood. She collected old clothing for needy families, arranged to have people come in and cook for the elderly and the infirm, lobbied businesspeople for donations on behalf of those who were living through the winter months without gas or electricity, and generally tried to connect impoverished families with those who had the means to help them. Parks also served as vice-president of her block club, an organization dedicated to improving the neighborhood and forming a youth program for recreation and job training; as vice-president of the Women's Auxiliary of the Detroit NAACP; and as a member of the United Sisterhood of Detroit, an interfaith group. In addition to her job and volunteer positions, Parks continued to travel and speak about the bus boycott and the civil rights movement. Whenever there was a civil rights convention or demonstration or march, Parks would return to the South to participate.

NO REST FOR THE MOVEMENT

With great pride, Parks watched the grassroots movement that she had helped spur into existence grow. While the MIA and the WPC evolved into service organizations to help black people in

IN HER OWN WORDS...

Rosa Parks stated candidly in an interview published by the Academy of Achievement:

I do the very best I can do to look upon life with optimism and hope and looking forward to a better day, but I don't think there is anything such as complete happiness. It pains me that there is still a lot of Klan activity and racism. I think when you say you're happy, you have everything that you need and everything that you want, and nothing more to wish for. I haven't reached that stage yet.

Montgomery, a new group, the Southern Christian Leadership Conference (SLC), headed by King and cofounded by him and several other southern ministers, was seeking to transform the struggle in Montgomery into a national crusade for black equality and even, in King's words, "a battle for the oppressed people of the world."

Other southern blacks had started to challenge their cities' segregation laws, and young black students were beginning to organize for change. With the encouragement of King and Ella Baker, an outspoken founder of SCLC, students across the South organized into the Student Nonviolent Coordinating Committee (SNCC). Among other activities, these young men and women met King's challenge "to take the freedom struggle into every community in the South without exception," by sitting in at segregated lunch counters and refusing to leave until they were served or arrested. Founded by James Farmer, the Congress of Racial Equality (CORE) furthered the cause of integration through nonviolent protest by sponsoring Freedom Rides—bus trips by integrated groups through the South on interstate carriers for the purpose of, in Farmer's words, challenging "every form of segregation met by the bus passenger." (Segregation was still prevalent in interstate bus terminals.)

Though Parks worked with the Detroit branches of both SNCC and CORE, she was not a supporter of nonviolence in all situations. "We [her family] always felt that if you talked violently and said what you would do if they did something to you, that did more good then nonviolence," she wrote in *My Story.*

King, on the other hand, demonstrated total acceptance of nonviolence in every aspect of his life. His strong beliefs were all the clearer when attending an SCLC convention in the autumn of 1962 in Birmingham, Alabama, a city known as "the cradle of segregation," she watched in horror as a white man in the audience, a member of the American Nazi party, jumped on the stage and began to pummel King with his fists. At first, King instinctively raised his arms to defend himself. But then, in the spirit of passive resistance, he dropped his arms to his sides. This so surprised his attacker that he ceased his assault just long enough to be wrestled into submission by onlookers. King refused to press charges. Parks too believed that nonviolence could be effective when practiced on a massive scale, as in the Montgomery bus boycott, and yet she also felt there were many situations on an individual level when it was impractical and could be mistaken for cowardice.

On August 28, 1963, Parks took part in the March on Washington, where King delivered his famous "I Have a Dream" speech to a cheering crowd of an estimated 250,000 people. No doubt Parks and other female leaders in the Movement supported the event, yet they felt the role women played in civil rights was being overlooked in the scheduled program. A. Philip Randolph got wind of the problem and arranged to introduce several notable females, although none were asked to speak. Parks accepted her welcome quietly when introduced by Randolph as part of this special tribute. Lena Horne was the sole woman to utter a word on stage when she shouted "Freedom." Still to its participants, the march (and subsequent events, such as Parks's appearance, that same autumn, at an SCLC conference in Richmond, Virginia, for the bestowal of its annual Rosa Parks Award) was a joyous, optimistic affirmation of the moral rightness of the cause of black equality and a celebration of the seeming inevitability of significant social change, but in a short time the depth of resistance to such reform was demonstrated anew.

Just 18 days after the march, a bomb planted by white supremacists at the Sixteenth Street Baptist Church in Birmingham killed four young black girls who were attending Sunday school. The bombing was only the latest in a long series of similar attacks by white supremacists against black churches, institutions, and individuals. Meanwhile, King and other civil rights leaders were under heavy surveillance by the FBI, and King even received threatening letters from the FBI suggesting that he commit suicide or risk having evidence of certain sexual indiscretions, obtained through illegal wiretaps, released to the public. The FBI's director, J. Edgar Hoover, publicly referred to King as the "most notorious liar" in America and "one of the lowest characters in the country."

Though President Lyndon Johnson signed a civil rights bill in 1964 that outlawed racial discrimination in employment and public places, authorized the federal government to sue to desegregate schools, and allowed the withholding of federal funds from programs that were administered discriminatorily, the legislation left large areas of concern essentially unaddressed. The most important of these was the issue of voting rights. In much of the South, intimidation and fraud were still being used to prevent blacks from registering and voting. This form of injustice was especially evident in Alabama, and in the spring of 1965, King and the SCLC planned a 50-mile march along Highway 80 from the small city of Selma, a city notorious for its violent resistance to black suffrage. Marchers were destined for the state capital in Montgomery to protest discriminatory voter registration practices. Parks, then 52, was invited to return to Montgomery as a participant during the last lap of the protest march.

After her flight from Detroit, Parks joined the 50,000 other marchers eight miles from Montgomery on March 25. Initially, her presence made her feel as if she were no longer vitally involved with the movement. No one seemed to recognize her, she had trouble keeping up, and as she was not wearing a jacket of the right color (the marchers had color-coordinated clothing), the protest organizers kept pulling her out of the column and placing her by the roadside. But as the protesters approached the capital, Parks was asked to step forward and march with King in the first row that was being captured for eternity by an increasing number of photographers. "I have love in my heart," Parks said when, in the shadow of the state capitol building—the so-called Cradle of the Confederacy—she was introduced to her fellow marchers and a large crowd of hostile, jeering onlookers.

Several months later, on August 6, 1965, Parks sat with King and several other civil rights figures at the Capitol in Washington, D.C., and witnessed the president signing the Voting Rights Act into law. The legislation guaranteed the rights of all citizens to register to vote without fear of discrimination, and outlawed literacy tests including the 21 questions used by registrars to prevent blacks from voting. One of the most tangible positive results of the civil rights movement, the Voting Rights Act of 1965 caused a great upward surge in black voter registration—an increase of 50 percent between 1964 and 1968 alone. (During that same time, for example, black voter registration in Mississippi alone jumped from 22,000 to 285,000.) (For additional information on this legislation, enter "Voting Rights Act" into any search engine and browse the sites listed.)

IN POLITICS

The rise in black voters led inevitably to an increase in the number of blacks seeking public office. In 1964, John Conyers, a black man, was elected to the U.S. House of Representatives from Michigan's First Congressional District. Conyers had asked for Parks's endorsement but received more. She volunteered to help his campaign in the primaries to the point of coaxing Martin Luther King, Jr. out of, she says, a long-held reservation not to endorse any candidate. King lent his verbal support in a Detroit rally on Easter weekend. With King and Parks in his corner, a relatively unknown Conyers edged out the field of six other Democrats. From there he easily beat his Republican opponent in the final election.

"King's crucial statement on my behalf quadrupled my visibility in the Black community," Conyers stated. "Therefore, if it wasn't for Rosa Parks, I never would have gotten elected." After his election Parks went to work for him as a receptionist and assistant in his Detroit office, where she concentrated on finding housing for Detroit's homeless. "Rosa Parks was so famous that people would come by my office to meet her, not me." Conyers recalled. "It was incredible."

Parks regarded Conyers's election and her own work as an important first step in providing Detroit's black population

John Conyers

John Conyers, Jr., was age thirty-five, a partner in the law firm Conyers, Bell and Townsend, and referee in Michigan's Compensation Department when he, in 1964, ran for the U.S. Congress. He competed in the primaries against a large Democratic field in the newly formed First District of Detroit. Young, articulate, and determined to see social and economic justice for all people, he, after becoming a known entity, was favored slightly over his more traditional opponents. He won that election and of course, every one since to return to the Congress for twenty terms.

Familiar with the workings of the Congress from a prior stint as Rep. John Dingell's legislative assistant, Conyers wasted no time making his mark as "Mr. Civil Liberty." He promoted Medicare and the voting rights bills, and opposed the Vietnam War. After all his campaign slogan had been "Jobs, Justice, Peace."

His legacy in the freedom arena was solidified by sponsoring the Hawkins-Humphrey Full Employment Bill and the Civil Rights Restoration Bill. He stood on the side against the death penalty and for law enforcement and jury reform to achieve a more equitable and safer outcome for Americans. He added an amendment to the Anti-Apartheid Act that prohibited export of nuclear materials, technology, equipment and information to or for South Africa. He sponsored the Martin Luther King Holiday Bill, Motor Voter Bill of 1993, Violence Against Women Act of 1994, and was a driving force behind the Help America Vote Act of 2002. He introduced the Military Tribunal Authorization Act II and Federal Bureau of Investigation Reform Act also of 2002.

Conyers is the ranking member of the House Judiciary Committee and Dean of the Congressional Black Caucus, which he helped found in 1969.

with the leadership and institutional organization (of the kind provided in Montgomery by the city's black ministers) that she felt it lacked, a need that was most clearly demonstrated by the violent riots that convulsed the city in 1967. She thought Conyers and other Black elected officials could be the voice of the disenfranchised and become the African-American leaders of tomorrow.

OVERCOMING GRIEF

On April 4, 1968, Parks and her mother were listening to the radio when they heard an announcement that King had been shot while organizing a march for black garbage workers who were striking in Memphis, Tennessee. Although news of an earlier attempt on King's life (in New York City in the summer of 1958) had at the time left Parks distraught, she responded to the first reports of the latest attack with greater equanimity. Parks was no longer shocked by the amount of hatred that the black fight for equal justice could arouse, and King himself had said that "a man who won't die for something is not fit to live." Still, when the news of his death came over the radio, she and Leona cried together for a long time. Parks then flew to Memphis with her friend and travel companion Louise Trappes to participate in the march supporting the sanitation workers that King could not attend. Noted singer and actor Harry Belafonte, later, took her to Atlanta for King's funeral.

King's death marked the beginning of a long period of sorrow for Parks. In the early 1970s, her husband, mother, and brother all became ill with cancer. For a time, she visited three different hospitals daily to see them, and caring for them required her to reduce her hours at work from full- to part-time. After five years of throat cancer, Ray Parks died in 1977; her brother, Sylvester, victim of stomach cancer, died three months later. By this time, her mother had become so weak from cancer that Rosa was forced to place her in a nursing home, where for a year Rosa visited her every day for breakfast, lunch, and dinner. In 1978, when Parks, who was then 65, moved into an apartment building for senior citizens, she moved her mother in with her and cared for her at home until the following year, when Leona McCauley died at age 91.

Though the death of so many of her loved ones was obviously a tremendous strain for Parks, she continued to stay busy with her work and volunteer duties. Long-time friend Elaine Steele was at her side caring for her like a daughter. "It just doesn't seem that an older person like I am should still have to be in the struggle," Parks said, "but if I have to be in it, then I have no choice but to keep on." Parks even began a sort of second career as a public figure, using her influence and reputation as the "first lady of civil rights" and the "mother of the freedom movement" to guide young people growing up in the crime-ridden neighborhoods of Detroit, and making frequent appearances at Detroit schools to talk to students and teach them to be proud of themselves. One Detroit school was called the Rosa Parks School in her honor, and 12th Street was renamed Rosa Parks Boulevard, as was Cleveland Avenue in Montgomery, where she had boarded the bus for her fateful ride.

In 1980, Parks became the first woman to receive the Martin Luther King, Jr., Nonviolent Peace Prize. With all the awards and accolades, she has never adjusted to the idea of celebrity. She says her place in the civil rights movement has grown larger with time. "I have more honorary degrees and plaques and awards than I can count, and I appreciate and cherish every single one of them," she stated in her autobiography. "But I have never gotten used to being a 'public person.'" Steele eventually managed the media contacts for her and sought payment for her appearances to build Parks's retirement nest egg.

That same year, 1980, *Ebony* magazine honored her as the living black woman who had done the most to advance the cause of civil rights. In 1985, she attended a reunion of her

Though she faced hardships, through the 1960s and 1970s, Parks continued to be an integral part of the movement she had helped spur into existence. Here, Parks (center) stands on the steps of the Dexter Avenue Baptist Church in Montgomery, Alabama, with SCLC president Ralph Abernathy and Coretta Scott King on December 5, 1975, the twentieth anniversary of her refusal to give up her bus seat.

class at Miss White's School in Montgomery, and four years later she returned for the dedication of the Civil Rights Memorial. The memorial bears the names of 40 men and women killed in the civil rights movement. It consists of a circular black granite table in front of a curving wall; water cascades down the wall onto the table, forming a thin film over the names and these words from the Old Testament Book of Amos, quoted often by King: "Until justice rolls down like water and righteousness like a mighty stream." In the late 1980s, Rosa extended her activism to the antiapartheid movement, was elected to the board of directors of the Detroit branch of the NAACP, and, in 1988, joined Jesse Jackson on the platform at the Democratic National Convention in Atlanta. But Parks's proudest achievement has been the establishment of the Rosa and Raymond Parks Institute for Self-Development, which she and Steele founded in 1988 after her retirement from Congressman Conyers's office.

9

Work to Do

Endowed initially with $10,000 Parks had received for an award, the Rosa and Raymond Parks Institute for Self-Development is a nonprofit organization that offers scholarships to young people and encourages them through communication and economic skills, current events, and health awareness, to develop self-esteem and become a positive influence on society. Parks, without children of her own, has always made the broader community of youth her focus. The institute provides the chance to pursue those interests in shaping productive citizens on a large scale. "I would like them to have the same sense of hope, dignity, and pride that was instilled in me by my family and my teachers," says Parks in her memoir.

Primarily the Pathway to Freedom program teaches young people African-American history, and the related bus tour, for example traveling across the country all the way to Canada, gives the children an experience to remember. It adds a deeper, lasting feeling than can be garnered from history books and lectures about the brave acts of slaves secreting themselves on the Underground Railroad to their final destination in Canada and centuries of struggle since. It cloaks youngsters in the meaning that exemplifies Parks's life of defiance for justice and getting up each morning to place one foot in front of each other in her daily walk to freedom.

This field research differs each year but with an equally compelling focus takes kids ages eleven through seventeen away from the limits of their impoverished urban neighborhoods and into a world that they have seen only on television—The Great Plains kept safe by Buffalo Soldiers or Harpers Ferry where John Brown led a freedom army or Court Square where the modern civil rights movement, this time fueled by Parks and the masses, was ignited.

Nothing speaks to the fortitude and dedication of the children and adult chaperones on these trips more then the events of July 17, 1997, the day the program's chartered Rite Way bus veered off highway I-95, flipped on its side and slid down one hundred and fifty feet into five feet of Nottoway River water. The tour was south of Petersburg, VA, tracing an eastern Underground Railroad trail to Nova Scotia. Thirty-five people were on board at the moment of the accident, including twenty-eight students. One chaperone, Elaine Steele's nephew, whom Parks thought of as a grandson, was killed and the driver and four youths were thrown into a coma.

Parks flew to Virginia to embrace the living with her strength and encourage them to complete the journey. However, the decision to continue was up to them. They heroically chose to resume their four thousand mile, fifteen-state and twenty-two-city sojourn in honor of the caring chaperone who would not see Canada. Young Makia Gibson explained the decision this way, "I have to finish. Until we cross the river into Toronto, Canada, our program says we are not free. We have to press on for our freedom." Thousands of young people have discovered that same unshackled pride of accomplishment since the inception of Pathways to Freedom.

The Institute's Intergenerational Network is another favorite program of the students. In it, computer savvy junior high school students share their knowledge with residents in senior care facilities. With a little patience teaching seniors to surf the Internet and send E-mail inspires a nurturing bond between mentors. Thaijuan Williamson said after training Rosa Parks, the first program graduate, "It's by far the highlight of my life," and added, "She was quick to catch on."

Parks is thrilled about the success of her institute. "I'm hoping that we'll reach as many youth as we can and that they will be motivated, trained, and inspired to reach their highest potential in life."

HIGH ROAD

The fragile child from Tuskegee accomplished much over the years despite bouts of ill health. Parks's unstoppable behavior continued after a car accident in 1987. It held after a pacemaker

DID YOU KNOW?

Programs offered by the Rosa & Raymond Parks Institute for Self-Development reach a multicultural population with affiliated chapters throughout the United States, Canada, and the Bahamas. The national headquarters for this nonprofit institute is located in Detroit, Michigan, where Parks resides. The array of life skills offered to youth ages 11 through 17 consists of:

Budget management, communications, computer technology, critical thinking, economic development, etiquette, goal setting, health education, historical roots, human relations, inter-generation networking, journal writing, personal growth, political awareness, science, self empowerment, services production, spiritual principles, and technology.

was inserted to regulate her heart a year later. Following that surgery Steele made arrangements for Parks to winter in Los Angeles at the home of Leo and Geraldine Branton. Leo Branton is a well-known civil rights lawyer. Parks would swing into selective appearances and join the Path to Freedom from those restful, sun-laden vacations.

Her endurance sped Parks to Tokyo, Japan in 1994. There she discussed a global strategy of nonviolence with Dr. Daisaka Ikeda, president of Soka University. Their first goal became shining the philosophy of nonviolence on the twelve million members of Ikeda's Soka Gakkai International, which extended over one hundred and twenty-eight countries.

For a short time in 1994 her family and friends wondered if her work was done. On the evening of August 30, a drunken young man, Joseph Kipper, broke into Parks's residence while she prepared for bed upstairs. She followed the sound of a loud thud and a man's cries to the Institute offices on the lower level. The man she confronted claimed he had chased off the intruder and suggested a two- or three-dollar tip was called for. Thinking the best of people, Parks went upstairs to the bedroom to retrieve the money from her purse. He followed the trusting woman and demanded all her cash. Then he beat her when she refused his unjust command. She screamed for him to stop, but in the end she acceded by giving him the $103 in her purse.

Steele responded immediately to Parks's phone call for help, although the police did not arrive until fifty minutes after being requested. Parks was eventually taken to the hospital for treatment. Wanting to keep the public outrage in the proper context, she stated, "I pray for this man and the conditions in our country that made him this way." She added, "I urge people not to read too much into the attack." Her institute has a youth-oriented drug prevention program now to curb the underlying causes for such violence. Still, reason led her to move to the twenty-fifth floor of the well-guarded Riverfront Towers.

Rosa Parks was awarded the Presidential Medal of Freedom in 1996 for her work with the civil rights movement and her continued commitment to peace and justice. Parks, wearing the medal she received earlier in the Oval Office, smiles here after being introduced at the dinner of the Congressional Black Caucus Foundation by President Bill Clinton.

NEVER GIVING UP

Her new comfortable home made the perfect setting for further authorship. *Rosa Parks: My Story* was a best seller, and sharing life philosophies in a collection of writings that melded with her focus on youth seemed the next logical choice. Both *Quiet Strength* and *Dear Mrs. Parks: A Dialogue with Today's Youth* fit that objective. She presented President Bill Clinton with a custom leather-bound edition of *Quiet Strength*, inscribed to his recently deceased mother, during the California Democratic Assembly in 1995. The president was moved to tears by her thoughtfulness. Clinton and she spoke again in 1996 when she was awarded the Presidential Medal of Freedom and then in 1999 as he placed the Congressional Gold Medal around her neck. His words to onlookers were "In so many ways Rosa Parks brought America home to our founders' dream . . . We must never ever, when this ceremony is over, forget about the power of ordinary people to stand in the fire for the cause of human dignity." (For additional information on these medals and their recipients, enter "congressional gold and presidential freedom medal" into any search engine and browse the sites listed.)

Perhaps the most memorable of her political encounters was meeting her hero, Nelson Mandela, the acclaimed freedom fighter and then-president of South Africa. He stopped in Detroit during a 1990 tour of America. Parks had not been invited to the reception line at the airport and, in truth, did not think her hero knew anything about this ordinary citizen. Through the intervention of Judge Damon Keith, Steele maneuvered Parks onto the VIP line. Winnie and Nelson Mandela stepped from the plane and advanced toward the receiving line when tears filled his eyes in wonder. "Ro-sa Parks. Ro-sa Parks. Ro-sa Parks," Mandela's voice rose to a shout, "Ro-sa Parks." The two heroes fell into an embrace with the understanding and adulation of old soldiers in a common battle against racial oppression, though an ocean apart.

Malcolm Collum, senior conservator at the Henry Ford Museum, works on restoring the 1948 General Motors bus where Rosa Parks refused to give up her seat. Her act of defiance helped propel the civil rights movement to prominence and cement her role in history as an indispensable activist for peace and equality.

Entering Parks's apartment some years later on May 30, 1998, Steele discovered the American icon unconscious on the floor. Parks was hospitalized immediately and luckily survived another health scare. Since then Steele has been even more judicious about Parks's occasional appearances, thus giving her added time to read up on the latest events in civil and human rights and to enjoy the view from her spacious apartment overlooking the Detroit waterway and Windsor, Canada. Windsor was once an end station on the Underground Railroad for many a freed slave, a fact not lost on Parks.

Prepared to age in private, she has been seen breaking that rule at the year 2000 dedication of the Rosa Parks Library and Museum on the grounds of Troy State University in Montgomery, Alabama, and, in 2001, being wheeled into the infamous General Motors bus that changed the course of her life. The Henry Ford Museum has since restored the bus, which it purchased at auction for $492,000 and put on exhibit at the automaker's museum in Dearborn, Michigan.

Rosa Parks has walked a life of honor and dignity, one well highlighted in the television movie *Rosa Parks* starring Angela Bassett, which first aired in 2002; in the Teaching Tolerance documentary *Mighty Times: The Legacy of Rosa Parks* that was nominated for an Academy Award in 2003; as well as the monument planned in tribute to Parks on Belle Isle. But commercial recognition also comes with controversy. In the 2002 comedy movie *Barbershop,* Parks's nonviolent defiance on that Montgomery bus was used as a punch line in a joke. When the rap group OutKast used her name as the title in one of the group's hit songs, she once again had enough of feeling demeaned and is suing the rappers to restore her good name and hopefully gain better control over its future use. It is reported that the highly respected attorney Johnnie Cochran is spearheading her cause.

Her institute, a significant tool in the social justice movement of the information age, is the enduring symbol that Parks wants associated with her name and the legacy it represents. "There is work to do," said Parks in *Quiet Strength.* "That is why I cannot stop or sit still. As long as a child needs help, as long as people are not free, there will be work to do."

1913 Rosa Louise McCauley born in Tuskegee, Alabama, on February 4

1932 Marries Raymond Parks in December

1933 Earns high school diploma by attending Alabama State College

1943 Joins NAACP and becomes branch secretary; attempts to register to vote and is denied

1949 Becomes adviser to the NAACP Youth Council

1955 Is arrested on December 1 for not yielding her seat to a white man on a Montgomery bus and is subsequently found guilty of violating segregation law; Montgomery bus boycott begins

1956 Loses job at Montgomery Fair department store; reindicted for boycotting city buses; U.S. Supreme Court declares segregation on Montgomery buses unconstitutional on November 13; boycott ends December 21

1963 Honored at March on Washington; speaks at SCLC Convention in Richmond, Virginia

1965 Participates in Selma-to-Montgomery protest march; begins working for Congressman John Conyers in Detroit

1980 Becomes first woman to receive Martin Luther King, Jr., Nonviolent Peace Prize; honored by Ebony magazine

1988 Founds the Rosa and Raymond Parks Institute for Self-Development; featured at Democratic National Convention with Jesse Jackson; retires after 23 years working for John Conyers

1989 Attends dedication of Civil Rights Memorial in Montgomery

1992 Attends Democratic National Convention in New York City; completes autobiography *My Story*

1994 Life philosophy in book form, *Quiet Strength: The Faith, the Hope, and the Heart of a Woman Who Changed a Nation,* is completed; in Japan builds a global strategy at Soka University for spreading the philosophy of nonviolence

1996 Advice provided in written work, *Dear Mrs. Parks: Dialogue with Today's Children*; Rosa Parks Library and Museum opens at Troy State University in Montgomery, Alabama

1999 Awarded Congressional Gold Medal, Congress's highest award for civilians, by President Clinton for her activism in civil rights; Smithsonian commissions a bust of her for the permanent exhibit in the U.S. Capitol

2001 Celebrates her 88th birthday; visits the bus on which she kept her historic seat at the Henry Ford Museum

2003 Teaching Tolerance documentary, *Mighty Times: The Legacy of Rosa Parks,* nominated for an Academy Award

Altman, Susan. *The Encyclopedia of African-American Heritage.* New York: Facts On File, Inc., 1998.

Bauerlein, Mark; Branham, Charles R.; et al. *Civil Rights Chronicles The African-American Struggle for Freedom.* Lincolnwood, IL: Legacy Publishing, Publications International, Ltd., 2003.

Barnes, Catherine A. *Journey from Jim Crow: The Desegregation of Southern Transit.* New York: Columbia University Press, 1983.

Blaustein, Albert P. and Zangrando, Robert L. *Civil Rights and the American Negro A Documentary History.* New York: Washington Square Press, Inc., 1968.

Branch, Taylor. *Parting the Waters: America in the King Years, 1954–1963.* New York: Simon and Schuster, 1988.

Brinkley, Douglas. *Rosa Parks.* Penguin Lives. New York: Viking, Penguin Group, 2000.

Clay, William L. *Just Permanent Interests: Black Americans in Congress 1870–1991.* New York: Amistad Press, Inc., 1992.

Crisis Magazine. "Turn of the Century White race crimes engulf nation 1900–1908." Baltimore: The Crisis Publishing Co., NAACP, July/August 1999.

Estell, Kenneth. *African America Portrait of a People.* Detroit: Visible Ink Press, 1994.

Frieze, Kai. *Rosa Parks: The Movement Organizes.* Englewood Cliffs, NJ: Silver Burdett Press, 1990.

Garrow, David J. *Bearing the Cross: Martin Luther King, Jr., and the Southern Christian Leadership Conference.* New York: Vintage, 1986.

Hampton, Henry and Fayer, Steve. *Voices of Freedom An Oral History of the Civil Rights Movement from the 1950s through the 1980s.* New York: Bantam Books (Blackside, Inc.), 1990.

———, ed. *The Montgomery Bus Boycott and the Women Who Started It: The Memoir of Jo Ann Gibson Robinson.* Knoxville: University of Tennessee Press, 1987.

MacDonald, Fiona. *Working for Equality*. New York: Franklin Watts, 1988.

Meriwether, Louise. *Don't Ride the Bus on Monday: The Rosa Parks Story*. Englewood Cliffs, NJ: Prentice Hall, 1973.

Metcalf, George. *Black Profiles*. New York: McGraw-Hill, 1968.

Morris, Aldon. *The Origins of the Civil Rights Movement: Black Communities Organizing for Change*. New York: Free Press, 1984.

Parks, Rosa, with Jim Haskins. *Rosa Parks: My Story*. New York: Dial Books, 1992.

Parks, Rosa, with Gregory Reed. *Quiet Strength: The Faith, the Hope, and Heart of a Woman Who Changed a Nation*. Zondervan Publishing Co., 1994.

Parks, Rosa, with Gregory Reed. *Dear Mrs. Parks: A Dialogue with Today's Children*. New York: Lee & Low Books, 1996.

Powledge, Fred. *Free at Last? The Civil Rights Movement and the People Who Made It*. Boston: Little, Brown, 1991.

Sklnasky, Jeff. *James Farmer*. New York: Chelsea House, 1992.

Smith, Jessie Carney. *Black Firsts—2,000 Years of Extraordinary Achievement*. Detroit: Visible Ink Press, 1994.

Wilkins, Roy, with Tom Mathews. *The Autobiography of Roy Wilkins Standing Fast*. New York: Da Capo Press, Inc., Plenum Publishing Corp., 1994.

Williams, Juan. *Eyes on the Prize: America's Civil Rights Years, 1954–65*. New York: Viking, 1987.

WEBSITES

Academy of Achievement: Rosa Parks
www.achievement.org/autodoc/page/par0pro-1

CNN.com: Rosa Parks
www.cnn.com/US/9906/15/rosa.parks.medal/

Grand Times: Rosa Parks
www.grandtimes.com/rosa.html

NAACP
www.naacp.org

National Parks Service: *Browder* v. *Gayle*
www.nps.gov/malu/documents/browder_v_gayle.htm

Rosa & Raymond Parks Institute For Self Development
www.rosaparks.org

Stetson University College of Law: *Browder* v. *Gayle*
www.law.stetson.edu/courses/casedigests/browder.pdf

Time 100: Rosa Parks
www.time.com/time/time100/heroes/profile/parks01.html

Troy State University Rosa Parks Library and Museum
www.tsum.edu./museum/

ABOUT THE AUTHOR

Mary Elizabeth Hull attended Brown University and has a special interest in black and women's history. She is a native of Pomfret, Connecticut.

AUTHOR OF ADDITIONAL TEXT, LEGACY EDITION

Gloria Blakely is a graduate of the Howard University honors program and is an active member of the Philadelphia Association of Black Journalists in Philadelphia, PA, where she resides. She also has been listed among up and coming children's book writers in *Something About the Authors* by Gale Services and was bestowed two writing awards by the 2003 Philadelphia Writers' Conference. Among other works she is also the author of *Jesse Jackson* and *Muhammad Ali* in the BLACK AMERICANS OF ACHIEVEMENT series and *Condoleezza Rice* in the AFRICAN AMERICAN LEADERS series by Chelsea House Publishers.

CONSULTING EDITOR, REVISED EDITION

Heather Lehr Wagner is a writer and editor. She is the author of 30 books exploring social and political issues and focusing on the lives of prominent Americans and has contributed to biographies of Harriet Tubman, Sojourner Truth, Thurgood Marshall, Malcolm X, Frederick Douglass, and Martin Luther King, Jr., in the BLACK AMERICANS OF ACHIEVEMENT legacy series. She earned a BA in political science from Duke University and an MA in government from the College of William and Mary. She lives with her husband and family in Pennsylvania.

CONSULTING EDITOR, FIRST EDITION

Nathan Irvin Huggins was W.E.B. Du Bois Professor of History and Director of the W.E.B. Du Bois Institute for Afro-American Research at Harvard University. He previously taught at Columbia University. Professor Huggins was the author of numerous books, including *Black Odyssey: The Afro-American Ordeal in Slavery*, *The Harlem Renaissance*, and *Slave and Citizen: The Life of Frederick Douglass*. Nathan I. Huggins died in 1989.